SPORT UTILITY VEHICLES

THE OFF-ROAD REVOLUTION

DAVID H. JACOBS

TODTRI

This book was designed and produced by
TODTRI Book Publishers
P.O. Box 572, New York, NY 10116-0572
FAX: (212) 695-6984

Printed and bound in China

ISBN 1-57717-085-7

Author: David H. Jacobs

Publisher: Robert M. Tod
Editor: Edward Douglas
Assistant Editor: Don Kennison
Designer: Mark Weinberg
Typesetting: Command-O Design

Photo Credits

CHEVROLET
65 (bottom), 74, 75 (top & botom)

FORD MOTOR COMPANY
18, 26, 34, 47, 55 (top), 68

GENERAL MOTORS MEDIA ARCHIVES
6, 7, 19 (top & bottom), 22, 23, 27, 28, 30, 31, 35, 38, 39, 42, 53 (top & bottom), 65 (top), 66, 67 (top & bottom)

RON KIMBALL
4–5, 36 (top), 43, 46, 48, 49, 50–51, 51 (right), 52, 54, 55 (bottom), 56–57, 58 (bottom), 62, 63 (top), 72–73, 76, 78, 79

JOHN LAMM
8–9, 10, 11, 12, 13 (top), 17 (top & bottom), 24–25, 32. 33 (top & bottom), 4, 58 (top), 70 (top & bottom), 71

LAND ROVER NORTH AMERICA
16, 20 (top), 37, 60 (bottom), 69

NISSAN
44

TOYOTA
63 (bottom), 64, 77 (top & bottom)

NICKY WRIGHT/NATIONAL MOTOR MUSEUM
6, 13 (bottom), 14, 15, 20 (bottom), 21, 36 (bottom), 40–4, 59 (top & bottom), 60 (top), 61

Contents

Introduction

Not long ago, a certain American big-city mayor (who shall be nameless) was being ferried across town in his official vehicle, a GMC Suburban SUV, not knowing that he was being tailed by a pesky reporter. The reporter later claimed that he had clocked the mayor's vehicle breaking the speed limit, at some points reaching 72 miles per hour (115 kilometers per hour). The mayor fired back that it simply wasn't so, that at a speed of 72 mph in such a vehicle he, his driver, and his passengers would have been bounced around inside, which hadn't happened, and therefore the story was untrue. The next day, a GMC spokesman pointed out respectfully but firmly that, whatever the veracity of the story, it was a fact that the Suburban was so superbly engineered that its passengers would be immune to being bounced around at any speed.

The point of the story is twofold: one, that the sport utility vehicle (SUV) phenomenon is so widespread it can be used as an official government prestige transporter; and, two, that a machine that had started as a rugged off-road trailblazer has evolved to the point where its high-line models offer a ride that compares in comfort to luxury-class automobiles.

The SUV has become one of the most dynamic motoring forces of modern times. In the half century since its wartime origins as the battlefield jeep, SUVs have enjoyed astounding success and popularity, with sixty-five million of them currently active on American roads. At this writing, SUVs are crowding the twenty percent mark in their share of all U.S.

Introduced in the early 1990s, Chevy's four-door Suburban swiftly took pride of place in the luxury utility class, empowered by its now-standard 5.7-liter V-8 engine. Shown here is the 1993 model.

passenger vehicles. Interestingly, some thirty percent of all SUV drivers are female, evidencing the machine's extraordinary crossover appeal. And surveys show that SUVs are the overwhelmingly popular favorites of teenage boys and girls.

What makes an SUV? High ground clearance, low front and rear overhangs, and selectable four-wheel drive (4WD). Most cars have two-wheel drive (2WD), with engine power being transmitted to the two-wheeled rear axle, making them 4X2 (4 wheels, 2-wheel drive). Four-wheel drive supplies power to both axles, making it a 4X4 (4 wheels, 4-wheel drive). Four-wheel drive equals improved traction, an especially desired off-road feature, for driving through mud, ruts, and rugged ground.

The first 4WD vehicle, the great-granddaddy of them all, was built in 1904 by Amsterdam's Spyker Manufacturers. Other forebears include the 1930s Marmon-Herrington 4wd American-built medium-sized trucks, and the same era's Willys' four-cylinder econo-trucks, which could be considered the progenitors of one of today's hottest SUV groups, the compacts/minis.

The utility vehicle really came into its own, however, with the World War II 1/4-ton jeep, the fountainhead from which today's wide range of SUVs takes it source. That's where the story really begins.

A final note: While a 4WD vehicle is by definition an off-road vehicle, statistics show that of today's SUVs, less than five percent of them will ever be used for off-road driving. The ironic culmination of the off-road revolution has been to make the SUV one of the all-time favorite on-road machines.

FOLLOWING PAGE:
The MB standardized jeep was developed by the Willys-Overland company's chief engineer Barney Roos, who would go on to pioneer the machine's postwar civilian version. Shown here in the background is Utah Beach in Normandy, France, site of one of the D-Day landings—a reminder of the vehicle's battlefield origins.

Trucks and SUVs have always had a one-to-one relationship, with truck platforms serving as templates for a wide variety of utility vehicles. Leading truck maker GMC's origins predated 1940, but the company didn't get around to making SUVs until three decades later.

Jeep Wrangler, "king of the compact SUVs." Built on the basic platform of the CJ, which it replaced, it embodies the breed's military-utility roots.

Chapter One

Starting Up

It was a personnel carrier, versatile and popular, able to carry passengers and cargo across rough ground in hard weather. An able performer on-road and off, it could climb, tow, pull a plow, and carry out countless other tasks. *It was the horse.*

Yet there was no place for horses in the mechanized warfare of the twentieth century. That was why the jeep—a kind of a motorized workhorse—was born. It helped the Allies win World War II. After the war, over the next half century, the jeep and its progeny would create an off-road revolution—the SUV phenomenon that is one of the driving forces in today's motor world.

Battle Wagon

Blitzkrieg, they called it, the "lightning war"—fast, mobile mechanized combat employed so devastatingly by the armies of Hitler's Third Reich. American military planners took note, preparing for the coming conflict. In 1940, U.S. Army brass challenged automakers to design and build a much-needed battlefield workhorse, a fast, lightweight, low-cost scout car. And they wanted it yesterday, or just about. They set a forty-nine-day deadline for delivery of the prototype.

Rising to the challenge was the American Bantam Car Company of Butler, Pennsylvania. Bantam's Karl Probst and his engineering team built a four-man open car, a light reconnaissance vehicle with a four-cylinder engine and a four-wheel-drive system, just getting it in under the deadline.

Bantam's design blueprints were made available to Willys Overland and Ford, serving as a springboard for the models which they delivered two months later, in the fall of that year. Willys offered the prototype Quad, similar to the Bantam BRC but with more muscle, while Ford

This interior view of the 1942 MB jeep is a study in stark, functional simplicity. Its no frills utilitarianism allowed for high-volume, mass production.

The little giant that started it all, the World War II-era jeep. This 1942-vintage Willys displays the model's signature stamped metal grille and recessed headlights.

A profile view shows off the machine's characteristic flat hood and rugged, low-slung construction. The flat body panels were designed for quick and easy replacement under combat conditions.

weighed in with the GP, a BRC clone with a Ford tractor engine. Willys quickly followed up with the improved model MA, powered by their Whippet Go-Devil engine.

The MA got the nod, chosen by the Army as its basic version light recon car. Willys and Ford were contracted to mass-produce the vehicles, while Bantam was tabbed to make jeep trailers and other wartime materiel. The MA was militarized into the MB Standardized Jeep. The origin of the term *jeep* is a mystery. Ford's version of the vehicle was designated as the GP, a soundalike to "jeep." That's one theory. Another is that the name was inspired by the Jeeps of Jeep island, strange but likable critters who appeared in the "Popeye the Sailor" newspaper funnies.

The jeep 1/4-ton utility vehicle had a truck-style separate body mounted on a chassis. It was combat-ready, with a low profile and a high ground clearance. Its flat body panels could be quickly replaced, even under enemy fire. It could travel well in snow or mud, desert and jungle. Put a machine gun on it, and it became an effective fast light fighting vehicle. In every theater of war, wherever the American G.I. went, there went the jeep.

"The Sun Never Sets on the Mighty Jeep" was Willys' proud slogan— no boast, just fact. By war's end, there were some 640,000 jeeps worldwide. Allied Supreme Commander (and future president) General Dwight D. Eisenhower hailed the as jeep as a vital war-winner.

Then came victory, and the jeep came home to win the peace. By September 1945, Willys' prototype Civilian Jeep CJ-1A had already given way to the CJ-2A model, debuting at a base price of $1,090. It was eagerly snapped up by

Demobilized and in demand: Willys' 1947 Civilian Jeep CJ-2A's four-cylinder Whippet engine is open for inspection. Interior lights were installed to illuminate the engine bay.

The 1944 MB jeep is equipped with a dash-mounted gun rack, keeping the driver's weapon close at hand. Note that the vehicle's top speed is 50 mph, compared with the 40 mph top rate of the 1942 version.

*This sportily styled
1948 Willys Jeepster is
a forerunner of things
to come. The dress-up
model features chrome
detailing and a luxe
interior, while retaining
practical front and rear
fender extended mud flaps.*

farmers, ranchers, foresters, and others in similar occupations, many of them ex-servicemen who knew the jeep as a battle-tested friend, an old war buddy.

In the fall of 1946, Willys launched the Jeep all-steel station wagon, whose exterior metal ribbing and color scheme curiously counterfeited those of the genuine Woody-style wooden station wagons. At roughly the same time, Dodge entered the lists with its own rival Power Wagon. In 1949 Willys debuted the 463 station wagon, updating its previous 2WD Jeep wagon with an optional 4WD capacity. Dodge's Power Wagon and the 463 4WD Jeep Wagon were important entries in the quickly expanding 4X4 market, foreshadowing the Jeep Cherokee and Toyota 4Runner, among other midsize 4WD wagons.

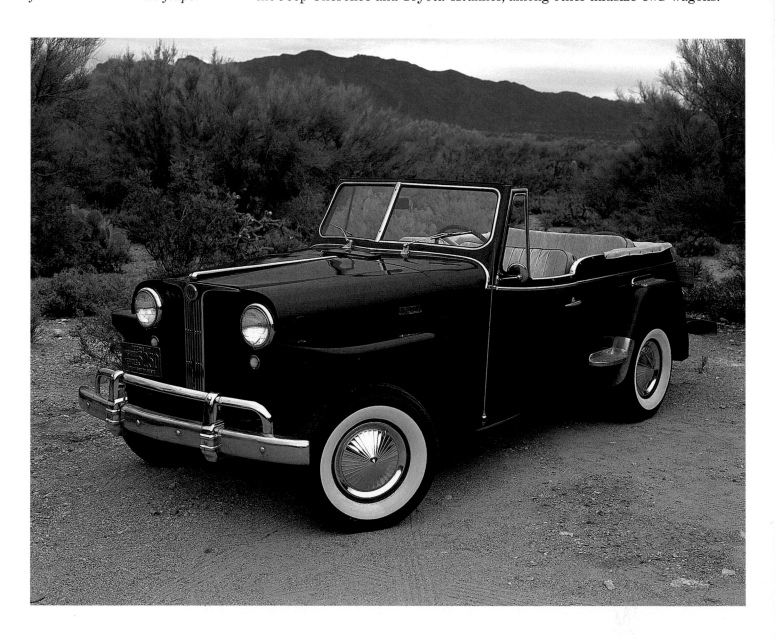

The Jeepster was the sport version of the Willys line. The 1950 version had a Hurricane F-head four-cylinder 90-hp engine. The one-piece wind-shield had become standard for all Jeeps in the previous model year.

Across the Atlantic, the British combined a jeep chassis with a Rover auto body, and *voilà!* the Land Rover was born. Officially debuting at the Amsterdam auto exposition of 1948, the Land Rover was the founder of a dynasty of internationally renowned, top-quality off-road vehicles.

Nineteen forty-nine saw the CJ-3A Universal Jeep, with a one-piece windshield among its upgrades. The next year the VJ2 Jeepster appeared, a sporty Jeep with a Whippet 134-cubic-inch four-cylinder L-head engine. The company used a Hurricane high-compression engine in some of its trucks, and a 90-horsepower Hurricane F-head engine soon became available as a Jeepster option.

During the early 1950s, Jeep built the next generation of military vehicles, the M38A1 1/4-ton truck. In 1953 the Kaiser automaking company bought up Willys Overland, changing its name to Willys Motors. The takeover was followed by the advent of the civilian version of the M38A1, the CJ-5, upgrading the platform with a Super Hurricane L-head engine and new axles and transmission. The watershed year for Willys was 1955, when all passenger-car production was shut down—ended. The future lay in the development of mass-market 4WD utility vehicles. One such was that year's 4WD Dispatcher, adopted by the U.S. Post Office and used by it in more or less unchanged form through the late 1980s.

The 1956 CJ-6 had a longer wheelbase and more cargo space than the CJ-5, but was otherwise the same. The CJ-6 never really caught on in the U.S. market, however, and was primarily sold abroad. Both models offered optional hardtops and 2WD and 4WD systems. An important feature was the Power Take Off (PTO) option, which harnessed the engine power to run such attachments as snow-plows, winches, and fence-post diggers. Such features help to explain why the 4WD utility vehicle concept was taking hold worldwide.

During the Korean War, Japan's Toyota company enjoyed success with its version of the jeep. In 1958 it entered the U.S. truck market with its pioneering FJ25 Land Cruiser, a stark, no-frills version of the Jeep CJ, with one important difference: instead of CJ's standard four-cylinder engine, the Land Cruiser sported a more powerful in-line-six cylinder block. Toyota's entry into the American 4X4 market caused barely a ripple among domestic manufacturers at the time, but it was the shape of things to come.

Meanwhile, Britain's Rover had ended its Series I Land Rovers in 1954, replacing them with the meatier engine and longer wheelbase of the LR Series II. With some upgrades, the Series II continued on until 1970. Top engineering and durability made the Rover a premium safari and expeditionary vehicle in the faraway places. It also attracted a fervent American following.

The late fifties was a boom time for recreational outdoor activities, a remarkable trend which continues to this day. Changing demographics and leisure-time demands would shape the evolution of the next generation of 4X4s, giving rise to the first true sport utility vehicles.

Taking its first bows, the British-made Land Rover debuted in 1948. Marrying a Rover auto body with a Jeep chassis, the result was similar to the 1946 Dodge Power Wagon. Jeep introduced its 4X4 wagon in 1949.

The 1948 Land Rover had selectable part-time 4WD capability and a starkly functional instrument panel. The steering wheel is on the left, according to Euro-style convention.

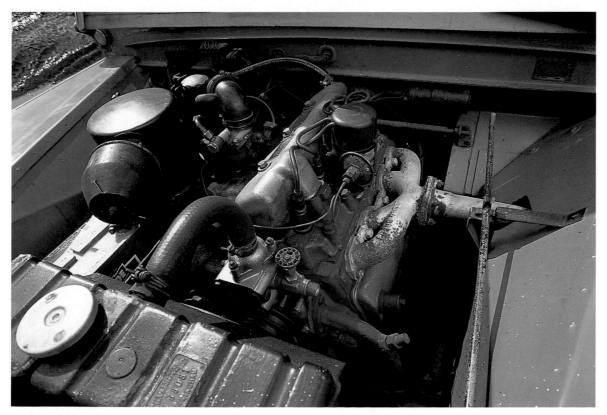

The little engine that could. The 1948 Land Rover Series I four-cylinder motor was the progenitor of generations of durable, smartly designed power plants.

*When the
Detroit titan,
Ford, entered
the SUV lists
it was its 1966
Bronco line,
based on its
Falcon and
Econoline
light-truck
platform, with
a 170-cubic-
inch six-cy-
linder engine.
Shown here is
the 1966 Bron-
co Roadster.*

Enter the SUV

A sporty note was sounded by the 1961 CJ-5 Tuxedo Park model. Named after a famed country club, it was a jeep with luxe trimmings, including chrome accents and whitewall tires. The next year's model upped the stylistics with a Parade Blue convertible top. A country club jeep! The old World War II veteran was going "society."

An expanding 4X4 market offered new opportunities. Toyota's successor to the FJ25, the 1960 FJ40 4WD Land Cruiser came in soft- and hardtop versions. International Harvester, famed for its heavy-duty farm equipment, launched its new 1961 Scout 800, first in a line of rugged 4WD vehicles.

In October 1962, Willys unveiled its important new J-series line of pickups and wagons, respectively the Gladiator and the Wagoneer. The Wagoneer's automatic transmission and 4WD options marked a milestone on the road to the SUV. It was powered by a Tornado overhead-cam in-line-six engine and fitted with the new J-series front suspension system.

This was a time for milestones. The military M38A1 jeep was replaced by the Ford-designed M151 recon vehicle, beginning a lengthy tour of duty. In 1963 Willys Jeep became Kaiser Jeep. The 1964 CJ-5 Tuxedo Park Mark IV was the glitziest special edition yet, bedecked in chrome doodads. Elegance was the watchword of the '65 Super Wagoneer, pitched to the luxury crowd with its gold-toned dual side trim panels, while sporting one of the brawniest engine packages yet, a four-barrel carte 327-cubic-inch V-8 with 270 base horsepower (bhp). International, too, debuted its breezy Scout 800 Sporttop in 1966.

Engine upgrades were the order of the day at Jeep, where the 1966 CJ-5 and CJ-6 now offered a "dauntless" cast-iron block V-6 engine opt, in addition to the standard in-line-four. Also available: bucket seats.

Chevrolet's initial entry into the SUV market was the 1969 Chevy K-10 Blazer, essentially a rear-enclosed 4X4 pickup truck inspired by the popular International Harvestor Scout.

The 1960s was a time of solid U.S. economic prosperity. As more families bought a second car, many chose a 4X4 for off-road adventures, such as camping, fishing, hunting, and scenic sightseeing. The definition of a 4WD vehicle was changing. Utility vehicles could do more than work, they could play. And they were fun. They filled and fueled an ever-growing demand for family leisure-time motoring. This need was at the heart of the sport utility vehicle phenomenon, which was about to really step on the gas.

Other automakers moved to supply that demand and occupy a section of the market niche. Mighty Ford's entry into the SUV field was the 1966 Bronco, which was not unlike the International Scout. Justly famous for its light trucks and pickups, Ford incorporated much of its Falcon and Econoline light-truck platform into the Bronco. There was a Bronco Roadster, SUV, and wagon, each powered by the light-truck line's 170-cubic-inch six-cylinder engine. The wagon featured a removable top. Bronco was Ford's initial entry in a line which would ultimately produce the Explorer, today's top-selling SUV in the United States.

The 1967 Jeepster Commando debuted in three versions, as a pickup, a convertible, and a wagon. It was the first compact 4WD vehicle to offer automatic transmission, another milestone of the SUV revolution, and a feature whose popularity grew geometrically long after the short-lived model was discontinued in 1973.

In 1967 Kaiser bought Buick's V-6 engine production facilities. The jeep's four-cylinder engine had been enough to fight World War II, but the civilian off-roaders of the mid- and late 1960s wanted V-6 power in their machines. By 1968, 75 percent of all Jeeps had V-6 engines.

The market could be volatile, though, as Ford affirmed when it dropped the Bronco Roadster in 1969, while continuing the pickup and midsize wagon models. Another of Detroit's Big Three entered the fray, as Chevrolet launched its 1969 K10 Blazer. Like Ford, Chevy's SUV entry sprang from a light-truck/pickup platform, and, like the Bronco, the Blazer would prove to be one of the big ones.

Minus its enclosed rear seat and cargo area, the 1969 Chevy K-10 Blazer shows its pickup truck roots. The vehicle was the product of the company's light-truck division.

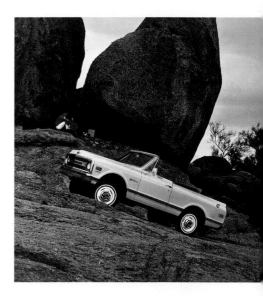

The closing decade saw industry stalwarts Toyota and Rover experiencing continuing worldwide popularity and building a small but growing following in the United States. Toyota's 1969 Land Cruiser went out with a dual-barreled carburetor F-engine. Rover was preparing the next generation to replace the long-running Series II LRs. In 1970 the Range Rover debuted, a full-sized 4WD wagon with luxury appointments, and one of the most popular models ever, continuing on virtually unchanged for the next twenty-five years. The 1971 Series III LRs would run for another fifteen years.

The 1950s had been the Jeep Decade, and the 1960s gave birth to the SUV phenomenon. Thus far the 4X4 had enjoyed a smooth and easy ride to ever-growing popularity, with every indication that the future would be the same, only more so. But other forces were at work, both industry-wide and globally, churning beneath the surface.

Like all other U.S.-made vehicles in the late sixties, 4X4 engines were fitted with mandated catalytic converters and similar anti-pollution devices which tended to adversely impact horsepower and performance. There was a growing awareness among trailriders for the need to follow some environmentally friendly rules while off-road, to maintain the landscape so all could continue to enjoy it. Nationwide events like the Jeep Jamboree rallies, and associations of off-roaders helped to spread the good word.

Rough Passage

In February 1970, American Motors Corporation bought Kaiser Jeep, splitting it into two entities: AMC, which would build civilian jeeps in Toledo, Ohio; and AM General, which would build military vehicles (including, later, the Hummer) at its South Bend, Indiana, plant. The change in ownership was an appropriate beginning for what would be a decade of transition—a time of trouble for Detroit and one of opportunity for SUVs.

Like Jeep, Rover built both civilian and military vehicles. Shown here is the British Army Land Rover Series III from the early 1970s.

The strikingly designed special edition 1974 Land Rover Desert Dream six-wheeler features a wrap-around, horizontally slotted front grille and dual hexagonal roof-mounted viewports.

The traditional metal front grille had been replaced with a plastic baffle grille by the time this 1974 Land Rover Series III military vehicle rolled onto the scene.

GMC introduced the original Jimmy with its removable hardtop in 1970. Though the GMC and Chevrolet truck divisions are both owned by parent company General Motors, both lines have maintained separate identities through the years.

Events began smoothly enough. The 1970 edition of the tortuous Baja 1000 off-road race was won by a Jeep. International rolled out its rugged 1971 model year Scout 11/800 C-class 4X4. General Motors' truck-making GMC division (separate from its Chevy trucks branch) adapted an existing platform into the new Jimmy 4X4, combining truck ruggedness with a fully enclosed rear seat and cargo area. The Jimmy was part of a history that went back as far as the jeep's. During World War II, GMC had built the U.S. Army's two-ton truck, the "Deuce-and-a-Half" of Red Ball Express fame, the original "Jimmy," as it was also called.

The SUV breed was being steadily improved and refined. The 1971 Jeep Wagoneer replaced its 232-cubic-inch in-line-six 145-bhp engine with a new 258-cubic-inch six-cylinder job, for a five-horsepower boost. The 1973 Wagoneer offered optional Quadra-Trac , a Borg Warner 4WD system that auto-adjusted power to front and rear axles, varying wheel speed for improved handling and control: an automatic full-time 4WD system, an important and ever more in demand feature. CJ-5 and CJ-6 continued, with CJ-5 performing strongly, notably in its Sport packages. But it was the end of the road that year for the Commando, as the compact 4x4 was discontinued.

Dodge used its successful Ram light-truck/pickup platform as a basis for its bow into the SUV sweepstakes with the 1974 Ramcharger, a 4X4 with luxury stylistics that belied its pre-production name: the Rhino. The next year, it was available in base and SE trim packages. The 1973 K10 Chevy Blazer had an optional full-time 4WD system; the '74 model had a removable top. The 1973 GMC Jimmy boasted an all-new exterior and an optional Sierra trim package, Sierra being the star of GMC's truck line. Ford dropped the Bronco pickup.

In the early part of the decade, some Japanese manufacturers, notably Datsun and Toyota, began making mini-trucks, filling a niche that was there by default. Detroit didn't want to make mini-trucks, and American buyers were largely uninterested in them. They wanted big pickups and 4WD wagons. But the mini-truck was fated to play a large role in the future development of SUVs.

The reason was the fuel crisis, which first made itself felt in 1972–74. Geopolitically caused oil shortages sent shock waves throughout the industrialized world. Many of the big trucks and pickups and 4X4s were fuel-inefficient. That didn't matter so much in a world of readily available low-priced gas, but by the end of 1974 that era had begun slipping away.

It would take time for the full effects of that changeover to make itself felt, but there were some early warning signs. International folded its line of pickups after the 1974 models, while a diesel-engined Scout was put into production. The fuel crunch was putting a big hurt on International and Jeep/AMC's light-truck line. Jeep's J-trucks were getting slammed, and even the full-sized Wagoneer was feeling the pinch.

The CJ models were what stemmed Jeep's slide. The compact CJ-5 was available in a variety of limited edition and custom engine packages, such as the 1974 Renegade, a bulked-up CJ-8 with a V-8 engine, sidebody racing stripes, whitewall tires and alloy wheels, and all the custom detailing.

The Cherokee

A vital launch for the company was the advent of the 1974 Jeep Cherokee, which positioned Jeep squarely in the middle of what was shaping up as a growth sector of the 4X4 world: the "prestige" or upmarket SUV. Again, here was where the utility vehicle was evolving into a kind of luxe 4WD family car. Unveiled to the public in October 1973, at the Cherokee Indian Reservation in

FOLLOWING PAGE: The original 1948 Land Rover Series I displays two signature features that would continue for decades: the grille-mounted headlights and the hood-mounted spare tire.

GMC, truck-builder to the United States, manufactured WWII's military 2 1/2-ton truck, the original "Jimmy." The civilian GMC big-rig hauler shown here is from 1941, the eve of wartime for America.

North Carolina, Jeep Cherokee was similar to the 1974 model year Wagoneer, except for its front grille (the kind sported by Jeep trucks) and a different rear taillight treatment. Cherokee debuted in two versions, a base model 16 and 17/S sport model. The standard engine was a 258-cubic-inch in-line-six with 110 bhp, and there were two optional V-8s, delivering 195- and 215 bhp.

Cherokee was an immediate success for Jeep, turning the tide against the damage wrought by the fuel crunch. The 1975 Cherokee Chief two-door 4WD wagon joined the line-up. The CJ-6, which had done well enough overseas but had never clicked in the United States, was discontinued, replaced by the CJ-7 in 1976, similar to CJ-5 but with a longer wheelbase and a number of structural improvements. Options included a one-piece poly-carbonate removable hardtop with metal lockable doors, vinyl door trim panels, and roll-down windows. Both CJ-models got new folding windshields, and their circular taillights became rectangular. Both CJs were available in Renegade option packages, with the CJ-7 Renegade being the first CJ to offer automatic transmission and Quadra-Trac full-time 4WD.

Competing for Attention

The fuel crisis wasn't a steady-state process. After the first shock, it slacked off and things went back to being more or less as they had been, except for the rise in prices at the gas pump. And they stayed high. Detroit kept on as before, with an occasional glance over the shoulder.

All the while, SUVs were tweaked, trimmed, and toughened. The 1974 GMC Jimmy got a new front end. The 1975 Ford Bronco came in a Ranger package, sharp-looking and

The 1973 Ford Bronco intro-duced the popular Ranger package, while the same year saw the dropping of the Bronco pickup truck. Bronco Roadster had been discon-tinued in 1969.

The stylish 1978 GMC Jimmy High Sierra package sported a front-end bull bar, roof rack, and rear-mounted spare. The High Sierra was available with a Casa Grande camper option.

scrappy. The '76 Chevy Blazer introduced its new roof design, replacing the removable hardtop with a permanent steel front t-cab.

Sport and custom packages were a plus. The 1977 Jeep CJs showcased the Golden Eagle Limited Edition custom trim option, a detailing design that must be hailed as a classic. There was a Levi package that featured interiors covered in that blue denim–style fabric. GMC Jimmy's top-line High Sierra trim package offered a deluxe add-on Casa Grande camper. The following year's Jimmy Desert Fox package evoked images of high adventure in the back of beyond.

Dodge's 1977 Ramcharger was a makeover model, and there was a Ram flat-bed pickup with a 4X4 package. The Ford Bronco Custom got a makeover into full-size status, and a removable hardtop. The 1979 CJ-5 marked that model's twenty-fifth birthday with a Silver Anniversary special edition with a silver finish and commemorative dashboard plaque. The CJ-7 Golden Eagle incorporated a unique composite hardtop. The CJ's standard engine at this time was a 258-cubic-inch six-cylinder engine with a two-barrel carte. Jeep Cherokee sported a new front grille and new rectangular headlights. The 1979 GMC Jimmy acquired a new Euro-influenced aero-styled front end.

The 1979 Scout 11/SS11 4X4 was the end of the line for that model, with production ending in 1980. After twenty pioneering years in the line, International was getting out of the SUV-making business. Many wondered who'd be next.

In 1979, the France-based Renault automaking company bought half of AMC in order to secure a foothold in the North American market. The decade had opened with AMC eating Kaiser Jeep, and it was closing with AMC being absorbed into a fitful tandem team with the French manufacturer: a pair of corporate takeovers that seemed to bracket the 1970s like rock-solid bookends.

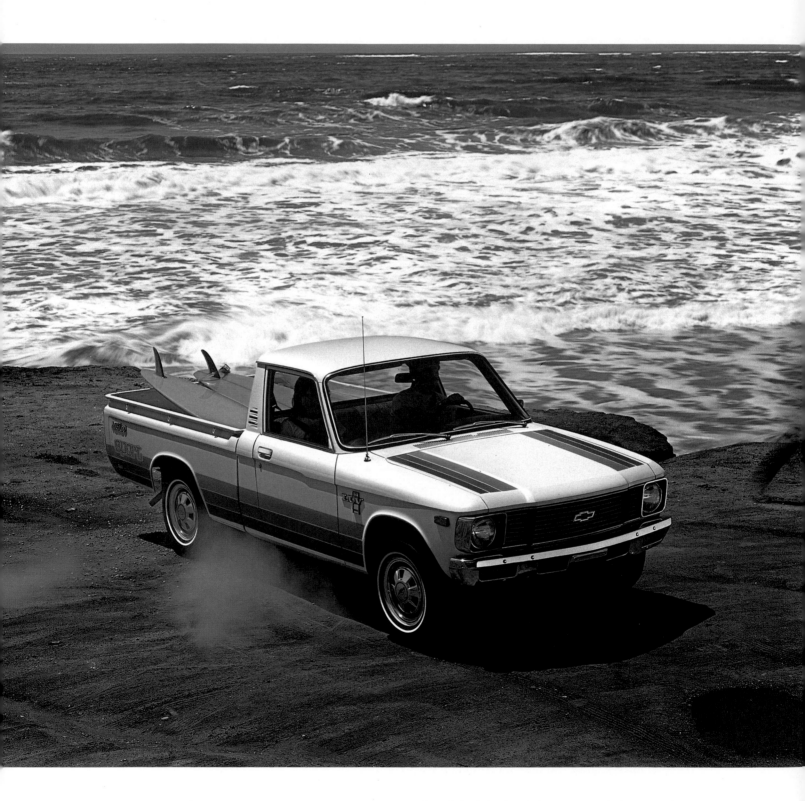

The global fuel crisis prepared the way for the 1979 Chevy LUV (Light Utility Vehicle), the company's entry into the burgeoning field of mini-trucks. The Isuzu-manufactured machine's production ended in 1982.

Cruising Speed

At the start of the 1980s, there were roughly twenty million light trucks, pickups, and 4X4s in America. In less than two decades, that number has tripled to an impressive sixty million vehicles, and much of the boom has been sparked by the SUV phenomenon. Those numbers would have seemed inconceivable to even the most far-sighted Detroit visionaries back in 1980, when the Iranian hostage crisis and Mid East tumult rocked the world with the second major oil shortage crisis. The results of that fuel crunch would permanently change the way Detroit did business, not least in the SUV line.

Taking a cue from Japan's successful lines of mini-trucks and compact SUVs, the Big Three of U.S. automakers—GM, Ford, and Chrysler—would eventually strike 4X4 gold by expanding into what might be called "full-spectrum" marketing, with an SUV for every age group and demographic category: from relatively low-priced compact SUVs for adventurous young singles, all the way up to the full-sized luxury SUVs which would establish their claim as the new American family car. But it would be a rough ride before that happy day was reached.

Rising Sun

During the middle and late 1970s, Japanese automakers continued to grow the market for their mini-trucks, the leaders in the field being Toyota, Datsun/Nissan, and Mazda. Throughout the history of 4X4s, there's been a definite one-to-one relationship between light trucks and SUVs, with the light truck serving as the platform for the resultant SUV, as can be seen in the genesis of the Chevy Blazer, Ford Bronco, Dodge Ramcharger, and many others. This same dynamic would be at work through the 1980s, with the Japanese mini-trucks inspiring new lines of compact and midsize SUVs.

The late 1970s were the heyday of the 2WD mini-truck. In an intricate case of cross-fertilization, Toyota used the Land Cruiser SUV platform as the foundation of its 1979 model year 4X4 4WD pickup, a well-engineered and instantly popular machine which in turn would inspire a new trend in SUVs later on in the decade, one which is still being felt. Automotive press and consumers alike hailed it as one of the best 4WD light trucks ever— rugged, dependable, and fuel-efficient. The 4X4 was available in an SR5 Sport package.

At the same time, Toyota's flagship SUV, the Land Cruiser, was being upsized, with the 1979 FJ55 Land Cruiser wagon now offering such luxe options as air-conditioning and power steering. But it was the success of the mini-trucks which would inspire Detroit's own new line of compact light trucks, such as GM's S-truck and Ford's Ranger, which would serve as the springboard for the next generation of domestic SUVs.

Chevrolet entered into an arrangement with Japan-based Isuzu to manufacture the light utility vehicle (LUV), an early East-West alliance that was Chevy's entry into the mini-truck field. An interesting but short-lived experiment, the LUV lasted from 1979 to 1982.

Dodge, which had entered the decade by defiantly showing the colors with its 1980 Ramcharger Macho package, covered its bets by allying with Mitsubishi to manufacture the RAM 50 mini-truck, and, later, the Montero/Raider mini, which would eventually generate yet another SUV line.

Not to be left out, Ford contracted with Mazda to build Courier. Perhaps the most important result of these fledgling East-West alliances was that it gave Detroit valuable exposure to some of the new automotive and manufacturing technologies from Japan, a technology transfer that would ultimately re-shape the industry.

American auto sales were slumping, but SUV sales remained hot. Ford weighed in with the potent and newly redesigned 1980 Bronco, the third generation of the now full-sized SUV classic. The new Bronco was a makeover model, inside and out, with an aero-styled sloping hood and wrap-around bumper. All-new was its Twin Traction beam front driving axle, the first individual suspension in a full-sized 4X4 model. A 300-cubic-inch six-cylinder engine was standard. An eye-catching option was the Bronco Ranger XLT trim package.

The 1980 Chevy Blazer went upscale with its Southwestern-style Silverado trim package. Jeep's CJ-5 and CJ-7 became available that year in the luxe-styled Laredo trim, offering such amenities as chrome front and rear bumperettes, special door trim panels, a leather-wrapped steering wheel, and weather-resistant indoor-outdoor carpeting, topped off with a Laredo nameplate on the instrument panel.

The 1980 Jeep CJ-models sported a standard overhead-valve in-line four-cylinder engine. A sign of the times: a CJ became the first 4WD vehicle to break the EPA's twenty-miles-per-gallon (32 kpg) barrier. With world oil supplies vulnerable to political power plays, fuel efficiency was smart design—and good business.

Dodge Ramcharger got its makeover in the model year 1982, its sharp edges rounded off for a more aerodynamically efficient Euro-style, as well as a weight loss for a leaner, meaner machine. A highlight of Jeep's 1982 CJ-7 was the special Jamboree package, commemorating the Jamboree off-road rallies and conclaves which had begun in the 1950s and grown in popularity over the years. The Jamboree special edition package included hood decals, chrome-styled wheels, and a color scheme of topaz gold or Olympic white.

The British Rover remained a power with the continuing success of its Range Rover and Series III Land Rovers. Throughout the decade, the Land Rovers were grouped according to wheelbase

Interior view of the 1979 Chevy LUV demonstrates the convergence of the Japanese-made mini-truck with the coming generation of compact SUVs.

length, classified as the LR 90, One Ten, and 127 models, with the numbering standing for the length in inches of their respective wheelbases. The military version of the Land Rover was the universal field car of the UK's armed forces, serving in a role similar to that of the M151 in the U.S. Army.

As for the M151, that veteran workhorse had just about reached the end of its tour of duty. The contract to build its successor was awarded in 1982 to American Motors General, the military vehicle–making half of the two companies which had been split off from American Motors back in 1970, its civilian counterpart being AMC Jeep.

First introduced in 1969, Chevrolet's Blazer became one of many models used to counteract the threat to Detroit from Japanese competition. Continually upgraded and improved throughout the 80s, the Blazer remains popular today.

Mean machine. The military's all-purpose Hummer became available in AM General's civilian model ten years after its development as a fighting vehicle. In this four-door hardtop version, the machine's combat origins are evident in its low profile and wide wheelbase.

The new battle wagon was designated the High Mobility, MultiPurpose Wheeled Vehicle/HMMWV, a mouthful which was shortened to the more user-friendly Hummer. It was a four-wheeled, low-profile, high ground clearance machine powered by a General Motors 6.2-liter diesel V-8 engine with 130 bhp. The Hummer was designed to replace a number of military vehicles, not only the M151 1/4-ton jeep, but also the 1/2-ton Mule, the 1 1/2 ton pickup truck, an ambulance, and one or two other motor pool standards. The basic Hummer would serve as a platform for close to twenty different variations, including a mobile missile launcher.

Just as the jeep had been plowshared into an immensely popular civilian vehicle, the Hummer would eventually be available in a civilian version—but not for another decade.

Meanwhile, Detroit was gearing up a whole new line of compact SUVs to fight the battle for the hearts and minds of the 4X4-buying public.

Compact Attack

"Small is beautiful" was a popular catchphrase of the period, but Detroit had long been dubious about downsizing. It had shunned making compact cars, with the exception of the Corvair and one or two other noble failures. The market was ceded by default to the likes of the VW Beetle and the Japanese imports that the public was buying like crazy. The Motor City wasn't about to make the same mistake with compact and midsize SUVs.

The Hummer's interior has plenty of elbow room, thanks to its wide wheelbase, but not much head room due to its combat-ready low ceiling.

AM General's Hummer presents its GM built V-8 engine, available in 6.2- or 6.5-liter diesel versions, with 170-bph standard and 195-bhp turbo ratings.

The Chevy S-10 was a compact pickup, not unlike the Japanese mini-trucks. The S-10 platform now served as the basis for the new 1983 S-10 Blazer 4X4, a smaller, scaled-down version of the K10. Solidly engineered and fuel-efficient, it debuted in three trim levels, base, Sport, and Tahoe. The Tahoe would eventually spin itself off into a stand-alone model.

GMC's entry in the downsize-derby was based on its compact light truck, the S-10 pickup. It was platformed into the 1983 S-15 Jimmy, the "Jimmy Jr.," kid brother to the larger-scale original K Jimmy. The compact 4X4 was outfitted with a standard 2.8-liter V-6 engine. Quick and nimble, it had plenty of eye appeal, especially in its Gypsy Sport package. Its older sibling, the K-Jimmy, had gotten rectangular headlights in the 1981 model year, appeared only with a removable hardtop in 1982, and was available in Sierra and posh High Sierra trim in 1983.

AMC Jeep had not been idle. In a bold move, they had downsized both the 1984 Cherokee and Wagoneer. The smaller, trimmer, more fuel-efficient vehicles were the forerunners of a new class of SUVs: the sportwagon. It was a winning strategy. The new Cherokee was now the only compact SUV available in both two-door and four-door versions. Internally, it was a revelation—and a revolution in the making. The standard truck-type chassis/frame construction had been replaced by "birdcage" style unibody structuring—a gridded-steel, skeletal framework.

The 1984 Cherokee and Wagoneer both bore a standard 2.4-liter in-line four-cylinder engine with 105 bhp, with a V-6 option. The original full-sized

The compact craze continues. Just as the GMC Jimmy had spun off the Jimmy Junior, and the Blazer the S-15, so too did the Ford Bronco generate the 1984 Bronco II, based on the Ranger pickup platform.

Wagoneer stayed in the line, only now renamed Grand Wagoneer, with a standard 258-cubic-inch in-line six-cylinder engine with 115 bhp. Command Trac part-time 4WD and Select Trac full-time 4WD were available. The sportwagons were an immediate hit.

In a short space of time, the Jimmy had spun-off the S-15 Jimmy Junior, the K10 Blazer had done the same with the S-10 Blazer, and the Wagoneer and Cherokee had reinvented themselves. So, too, did Ford debut its compact SUV, the Bronco II, in 1984. Bronco II was launched on a compact light-truck platform, that of the Ranger pickup. It came in three levels of trim: base, XLT, and the luxury-class XLS.

The near-simultaneous launch of the compact SUVs came at a critical time for Detroit. Now, almost two decades later, the continuing availability of a steady supply of reasonably affordable gas is taken for granted (so far!). Such was not the case in the early 1980s. Compact was in demand, but Detroit's early attempts to compete globally in the compact car market performed spottily at best. But the downsized SUVs were hot sellers, restoring much needed confidence and cash. The American automotive colossus had shown that it could adapt to a time of technological transition, survive, and thrive.

Change cuts both ways, however, not only giving, but just as frequently taking away. The 1985 Jeep CJ-5 was the last of the breed. The model, which had debuted in 1954, was now discontinued. CJ fans could find some consolation

A brace of 1983 Chevy Blazers: on the left, the smaller S-10 Blazer, making its debut that year; on the right, the full-size K-10 model.

In the early '80s there were about 20 million light trucks, 4X4s, and pickups in the United States. Today that number has tripled with machines like this 1986 Chevrolet pickup adding to the total.

Debuting in 1970, the Range Rover was one of the first of the "leisure 4X4s," with its design remaining more or less unchanged for the following twenty-six years. The 1987 Range Rover shown here is equipped with a turbo diesel engine.

in the CJ-7's new standard 2.5-liter four-cylinder engine. But not for long. The 1986 CJ-7 would be the last of its line.

Dodge Ramcharger highlighted its appeal with a variety of custom options in the 1985 model year, including Royal SE and custom trim and the Prospector package. The following year saw Ramcharger fitted with a new grille. One of the most enduringly popular and stylish custom packages was first introduced in the 1985 Ford Bronco Eddie Bauer trim option, designed by the world renowned maker of outdoors attire. Bronco II was soon available in the Bauer package, while dropping the XLS option in 1986.

In response to the S-15 Jimmy and the S-10 Blazer (and later Bronco II) which had been a response to Japan's mini-trucks—came the 1984 Toyota 4Runner. Built on a mini-truck's tough 4X4 chassis, it was a utility vehicle with a pickup-style canopy enclosing a rear seat and stowage, and was one tough customer. It was made even more attractive the following year by the addition of an auto-locking feature on the front hubs when the 4WD was engaged, a feature available on all Toyota's 4X4 SR5 models. The 4Runner stood in the same "little brother" relationship to the full-size Land Cruiser as Detroit's compact SUVs had to their older siblings.

The 1989 Range Rover four-door wagon is fit for a country squire. Range Rover pioneered the use of the center differential lock to facilitate full-time 4WD as early as 1970.

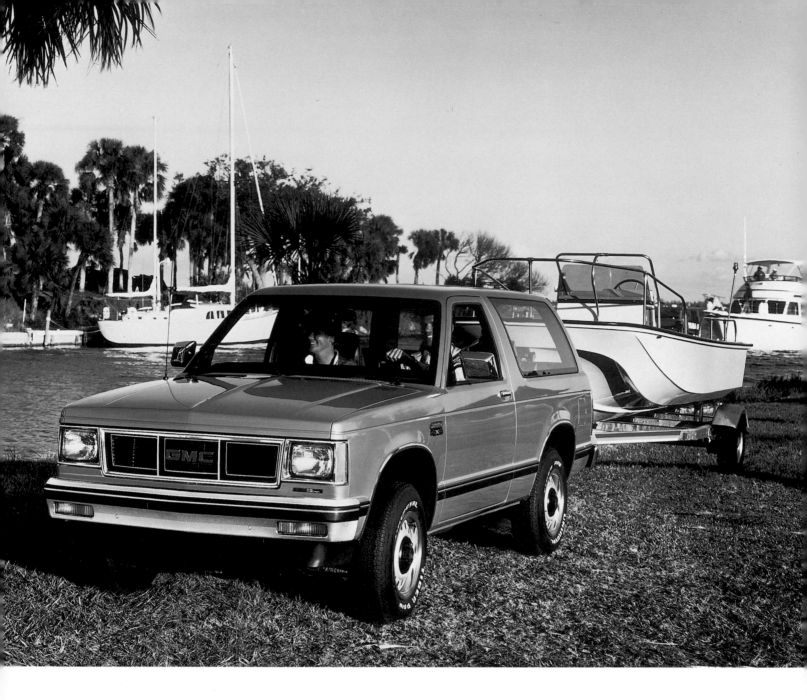

As the 1980s progressed, more and more people were eager to buy 4X4s, and automakers in the United States and Japan obliged them. Shown here is GMC's 1987 4X4 Jimmy.

Replacing the CJ-5 and CJ-7 in the Jeep lineup was the new 1987 YJ Wrangler. Elements of the CJ platform were evident in the vehicle, whose axles had been widened and its steering improved. The doors and endgate had been redesigned, and the five-spoke cast-aluminum wheels bore the Jeep nameplate. The rugged compact was available in optional Laredo and Sahara trim packages, the latter in desert-sands khaki or coffee-colored exteriors.

The 1986 GMC S-15 Jimmy got a newly redesigned instrument panel, while the following year saw the debut of its new Timberline trim option. The 1987 Bronco XLT showed a new aero-styled front end.

The 1988 Cherokee models bore a new and distinctive eight-slot vertical grille, a signature feature. Its parent company had gotten a new owner, as AMC was acquired by Chrysler, under the direction of Chrysler chief Lee Iaccoca. In one swoop Chrysler, whose share of the SUV market had been limited to Dodge Ramcharger, now owned Jeep with its enviable positioning in the compact, midsize, and full-size branches. (AM General, maker of the military Hummer, had already been split off from the parent company several years earlier, when it was acquired by the LTV Corporation, a defense contractor.)

The 1987 Chevy Blazer introduced
new aero-styling touches, and boasted
a newly redesigned instrument panel.

FOLLOWING PAGE:
Jeep Cherokee has enjoyed great popularity since its
early 1980 launch as the first sportwagon available
in two or four doors. This 1993 4.0 Limited features
a newly standard stainless steel exhaust system.

The 1989 Chevy Geo Tracker was an example of East-West cross fertilization, with the spunky two-door compact SUV being imported from Japan, and distributed in the United States by Chevrolet. Available in hardtop and convertible versions, the Tracker had a 1.6-liter four-cylinder engine with 80 bhp.

Off-road Rally

Nothing succeeds like success. The eighties decade pitched a lot of ups and downs at Detroit, but by and large the SUV trend kept booming. The public wanted 4X4s. New makes and models proliferated both here and in Japan.

Chevy decided that "If you can't beat 'em, import 'em," and marketed the new 1989 Geo Tracker compact utility vehicle, which was made in Japan. Tracker was a spunky two-door 4WD SUV with a 1.6-liter engine with 80 bhp. After the first year, Trackers were produced in Canada, and were available as convertibles or hardtops. On the home front, the 1989 Chevy Blazers came in a lustrous new "wet-look" painted exterior, available in a variety of color combinations. Within a year or so, most Detroit-made SUVs were similarly finished.

Ford Bronco II offered its 1988 model in a sharp XL Sport model. More substantive changes debuted the following year, with a new, redesigned front end aero-styling. The 1990 Bronco II added the XLT trim option; and the 1991 model? There was no 1991 Bronco II. The aging Bronco had been retired, put out to pasture, to be replaced by the forthcoming Explorer.

Dodge marketed its rebadged version of the Mitsubishi Montero, the 1987 Dodge Raider, for a short two-year span. Nineteen eighty-nine saw the Dodge AW150 Ram, while the 1991 edition Ramcharger got a new front grille. The Ramcharger in 1992 brought out a high-line Canyon Sport package, while the next year saw Ramcharger go out of production, ending Dodge's presence in the full-size SUV field.

GMC's Jimmy Jr. dropped the prefix from the 1990 S-15 and became just plain Jimmy. Its big brother was classified as the V-Jimmy, the 1988 models having been fitted with a standard 5.7-liter fuel-injected Los V-8 engine. The more compact Jimmy had a standard 2.8-liter V-6. SLX and SLE trim packages were available. The 1991 just-plain-Jimmy added a four-door option, a potent sales draw.

Jeep Wrangler debuted in 1990 the Islander package, whose striking sunset-orange graphics made it a natural for seaside resorts and as a beach car.

This custom studio Special Edition 1990 Lambo four-door 4X4 bristles with rough and ready ruggedness, sacrificing rounded aero-styling for squat, boxy dynamism.

One of the original compact import SUVs was the Nissan Path-finder, shown here in its 1989 version. The two-door sportwagon featured part-time, on-demand 4WD capability.

The 1991 Wrangler dropped the Laredo trim package, replacing it with new Renegade option, augmenting the standard 4.2-liter engine with an available 4.0-liter six-cylinder engine with 180 bhp.

The Jeep Cherokee and Wagoneer were also fitted with the 4.0-liter engine in 1989, only as standard equipment. The 1991 Cherokee offered a Sport four-door model and the top-scale Briarwood trim package. But it was the final year of production for the Grand Wagoneer, which was discontinued, though only to make room for its future successor, the Grand Cherokee.

Another milestone was reached on March 22, 1990, in Toledo, Ohio, as the production line rolled out its millionth Jeep, a red XJ Cherokee.

The 1988 Toyota FJ62 Land Cruiser had an upgraded fuel-injected engine, with an optional automatic transmission coupled with part-time 4WD. Land Cruiser was a four-door wagon, 4Runner was a two-door utility vehicle. The 1990 4Runner, based on a mini-truck 1989 pickup platform, was a luxe 4X4 available in two or four doors. The removable rear roof section feature was gone, rear anti-lock brakes were standard, and shift-on-the-fly 4WD was optional.

Another of the original SUVs was the Nissan Pathfinder, a two-door 4WD wagon. The 1989 edition offered on-demand 4WD and the shift-on-the-fly capacity at speeds of less than 25 mph (40 kph). The 1990 Pathfinder became available in four doors, and in the following year the two-door version was done away with.

Mitsubishi's 1989 Montero two-door SUV was upgraded into a new four-door body style and empowered with a new V-6 engine similar to that of the Dodge

Caravan. A 4-cylinder engine was standard on the two-door models. Part-time 4WD was standard on all models.

Isuzu's midsize Trooper 4X4 was joined in model year 1989 by the mini-SUV short-wheelbase Trooper II. Also taking its first bows for the company was the new Amigo convertible utility vehicle in two-door and four-door versions, with two different four-cylinder engine options.

The short-wheelbase Trooper II was discontinued the following year, however. Its failings may have been not unlike those of the Suzuki Samurai, a two-door luxe 4WD utility vehicle convertible and hardtop. The Samurai got a knock for its alleged tendencies toward tipping when turning corners, and sales were ailing by 1988. Suzuki replied with the 1989 Sidekick, another mini-SUV, but with a more powerful engine, wider track, and a longer wheelbase for greater stability. The Sidekick caught on, and the 1991 edition added a four-door version to the original two-door model.

Subaru went in a slightly different direction, domesticating the SUV toward a more suburban family car styling, launching in 1990 the new Subaru Legacy, a four-door 4WD vehicle. Available in sedan or wagon models, it was powered by a four-cylinder engine, and is considered one of the first crossover or hybrid SUVs. All the elements were in place to create the next decade's global SUV phenomenon.

The 1989 Wrangler came in a variety of trim packages: base, Sport, Laredo, Sahara, and—shown here—Islander, whose sunset colors and graphics recommended it to the surfer set.

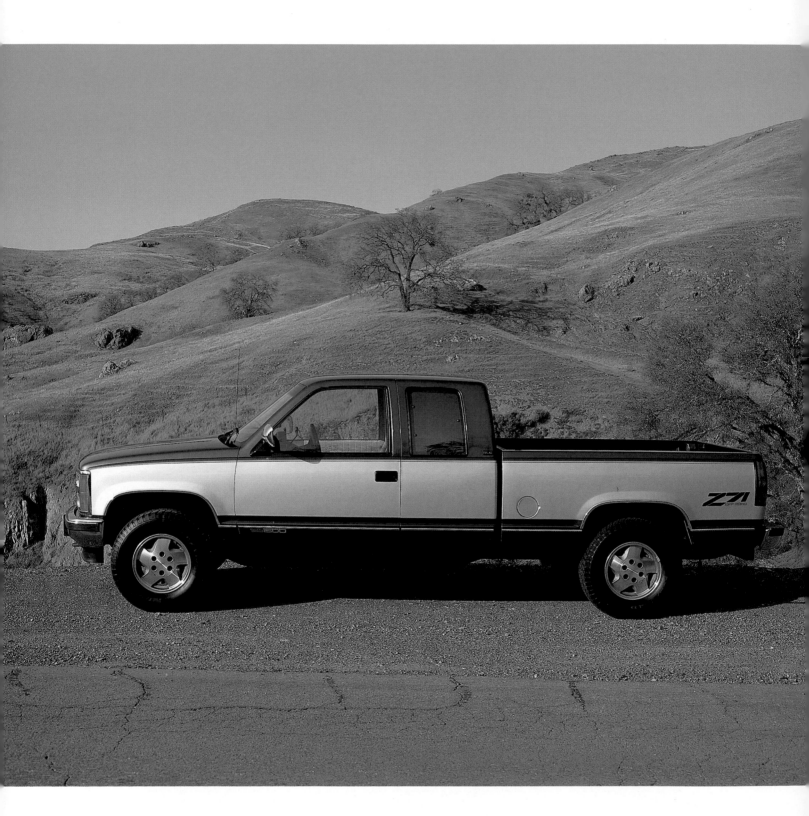

The 1993 Ford Explorer, powered by a 4.0-liter V-6 engine, began as a compact SUV and evolved into a mainstay of the midsize class.

Chapter Three

Full Throttle

There was power in the 4X4 concept, the power to constantly reinvent itself to fill yet more niches, and to create demand.

The WWII-era jeep had given rise to the sport utility vehicle. The SUV trend had grown to fill a wide range of marketing dynamics, from compact to full-size, from rugged to luxurious. They were already widely popular at the start of the 1990s. As the decade nears its end, SUVs are still among the dominant forces in the automotive world.

Jousting

By the nineties, Detroit had weathered some rough financial passages, some of the roughest yet. The crisis was past, but the competition was fiercer than ever, and nowhere more so than in the ever more high-profile arena of dueling SUVs.

A powerful entry took the field with the debut of the successor to Ford Bronco II, the 1991 Explorer. Explorer was leaner and meaner, more compact. It had a 4.0-liter V-6 engine and came in two-door and four-door versions. It debuted during the silver anniversary year of the original Bronco, which marked the occasion of its twenty-fifth birthday with a special edition package. Explorer would go on to enjoy tremendous success, becoming America's best-selling SUV.

The midsize Explorer came in two- and four-door versions, and had four trim levels: base XL, Sport, XLT, and the Eddie Bauer package. A new kind of sheet-metal construction went into the making of Explorer, which was built at the company's plant in Louisville, Kentucky.

Again demonstrating the linkage between light trucks and SUVs, Chevy's K-class pickup served as the platform for the 1992 K1500 Blazer, a makeover model with a complete re-style. Shift-on-the-fly 4WD was standard, while the diesel engine option was discontinued. Trim levels included Silverado and a new Sport package. The S-10 Blazer—available in four-door— served as the basic platform for the posh 1991 Oldsmobile Bravada 4WD wagon.

The 1993 Ford Explorer, powered by a 4.0-liter V-6 engine, began as a compact SUV and evolved into a mainstay of the midsize class.

GMC reinvented its full-size SUV with the introduction of the 1992 Yukon. Jeep debuted in 1993 its new Grand Cherokee four-door wagon in the ZJ luxury class, with an optional V-8 engine. *Motor Trend* magazine voted it Truck of the Year. A stainless steel exhaust system was standard on that year's Wagoneer and Cherokee.

Toyota nudged the 1991 Land Cruiser up into full-size luxury-class status with this makeover model of the four-door 4WD wagon. It had been re-engineered upward with coil springs replacing leaf springs and permanent 4WD. It had a 4.0-liter in-line-six engine with 155 bhp. The 1992 4Runner had a new grille and front bumper, and new aero-styled headlights. A V-6 engine was optional. The next year, though, the two-door 4Runner was dropped.

Isuzu's 1991 Rodeo was a new pickup-based SUV, built at a South Bend, Indiana plant. Rodeo had a standard four-cylinder engine and an optional V-6. Its long wheelbase was designed for greater roadability and smooth-riding

This customized 1992 GMC Z71 pickup truck sports sleek chrome detailing and five-spoke alloy wheels. The rear half-cab feature has been incorporated into many of the SUVs of the present generation.

GMC's short-lived Typhoon with its 280-bhp Turbo
engine was a forerunner of the full-size 1992 two-
door Yukon, shown here in a striking trim package.

comfort. The franchise at Isuzu was the Trooper, which got a bulkier make-over in its 1992 model year, beefing up into the full-size class. Muscle needs power, which was provided courtesy of a new standard single-overhead-cam 3.2-liter V-6 engine, with an optional LS package double-overhead-cam engine with 190 bhp.

Mitsubishi's 1992 Montero went the makeover route as well, with new wheels, a new grille, and a newly muscled-up engine with a horsepower boost. The next year's model had shift-on-the-fly 4WD and optional anti-lock brakes.

Back in the United States, Chrysler's AM General offered in 1992 the first-ever civilian model of the Hummer, possibly the supreme world-class 4X4, with a price tag to match: base price started somewhere around fifty-five thousand dollars. Hollywood titan Arnold "The Terminator" Schwarzeneggar bought one of the first to become available.

Arnold's got one. Bruce Willis has one. How about you? Quality costs, and the AM General Hummer base price of roughly $56,000 puts it up into the range of world-class luxury cars.

It's an endless summer for this studio-customized Special Edition Kenwood Jeep, complete with rollbar, alloy wheels, stylized front grille, and a vividly colored paint job.

SUVs Rule

Four-by-fours are generally adept at climbing hills, so it was no surprise in the mid-1990s when they began climbing into categories, and sales numbers, rivaling those of upmarket luxury cars and mini-vans.

The full-size SUV was seen not so much as a second-choice adjunct to the traditional family car, but as an alternative to it. After all, the SUV could do anything that a car or mini-van could do, plus it had 4WD off-road capability, even if more and more new owners were using the vehicles for their on-road driving needs. And the fully-loaded deluxe SUVs were second to none in the luxury class. At the other end of the 4X4 spectrum, the scrappy compacts and mini-SUVs were particularly attractive to young people, thanks to reasonable prices and a rugged design that facilitated an active lifestyle.

Chevy powered up the now-classic Blazer in its 1995 makeover model. It was an all-new, re-engineered S-10 Blazer, with the S-10 prefix dropped to establish that this Blazer was *the* Blazer. Blazer had a 4.3-liter V-6 engine with 195 bhp, and was available in two-door and four-door versions. Meanwhile, the full-size Blazer now became the 1995 Tahoe, with a newly designed interior and a 5.7-liter V-8 engine. The same year also saw the bow of the Chevy Suburban, biggest of all its full-sized SUVs, a posh fully-loaded machine for those who like their 4X4s luxe—and powerful, thanks to its V-8 engine.

Chevrolet's full-size Suburban occupies the summit of the SUV mountain, a luxury 4X4 that's on its way towards being the new upmarket family car of choice. Shown here is Bruce Canepa's custom Suburban in refrigerator white with black trim.

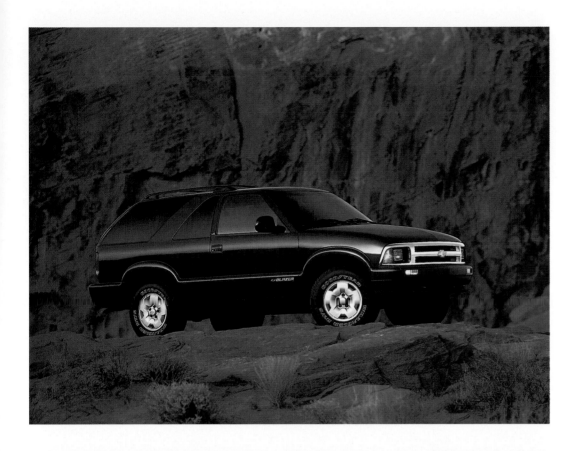

The 1995 Chevy Blazer was a makeover model, an all-new, revamped S-10-based platform, minus the S-10 prefix. Available in two- and four-door versions, the model was fitted with a 4.3-liter V-6 engine with 195 bhp.

The plush interior of the 1995 Blazer shows the model's evolution into a mid-size luxury machine, while still retaining plenty of 4X4 muscle under the smoothly appointed stylings.

Similarly, Ford's 1995 Explorer went the makeover route, enhancing the sizzle of an already hot seller with a newly redesigned exterior, including new front grille, new headlight and taillight treatments, and stylish new side moldings, in two- and four-door versions. The following year welcomed the AWD Explorers in XLT, Limited, and Eddie Bauer packages. The venerable Bronco was discontinued, but only to make way for the full-sized Expedition. The 1997 Expedition was built on an F-150 light-truck platform, and was pitched to compete with the Chevy Tahoe and GMC Yukon.

GMC's 1995 Jimmy was an all-new SUV based on the Sonoma light-truck platform, sparked by its 4.3-liter V-6 engine with 195 bhp. The midsized Jimmy and full-sized Yukon both continued to perform strongly in the marketplace, as well as in on-road and off-road venues.

FOLLOWING PAGE: Mood indigo—the 1997 Ford Expedition plays the blues. Ford Control Trac systems include an electro-select 4WD option.

Based on the F-150 truck platform, the 1997 Ford Expedition replaced the Bronco. This full-size, four-door SUV has a standard 4.6-liter, 215-bhp engine, with an optional 5.4-liter V-8.

The 1996 Ford Explorer demonstrates the rugged "off-roadability" that helped it sell close to 400,000 SUVs the following year.

The 1998 Lincoln Navigator, the prestigious luxury automaker's first SUV, is a sign of the times. Built on an Expedition platform, this chrome-fronted four-door seats eight and can tow an 8,000 pound (3,600 kilogram) load.

The 1996 Wrangler shines a light on the past with its new retro-look headlights, replacing the square lights that had been standard for decades.

It's not a mini-van. A 1996 Jeep Cherokee sport-wagon shows what four-wheel drive is all about, flashing its signature vertically slotted front grille.

Jeep's 1995 Wrangler SUV dropped the burly Renegade package, replacing it with the Rio Grande option. The 1996 Cherokee got an engine update, while the same year's Grand Cherokee was re-styled and repositioned as a threat to Ford Explorer, thanks to an improved V-6 engine and front suspension, and an overall upgrade. Grand Cherokee offered Selec-Trac 4WD and Laredo and Limited trim packages, as well as the Orvis trim option, styled by that well-known outdoor supply company for fly fishermen.

Originally positioned as a compact, by the mid-1990s the Cherokee had evolved into a midsize rival of the top-selling Ford Explorer, the leader in its class. The 1995 Cherokee Sport package option is shown here.

The 1994 Wrangler's treatment of the rear bumperette is pure WWII-era MB jeep design, as is the rear-mounted spare tire.

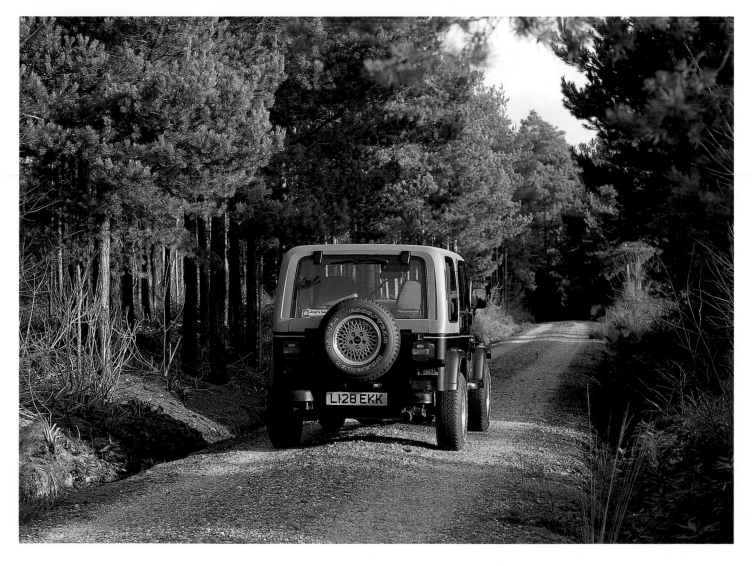

As it had done for decades, the UK's Rover company continued doing what it did best, namely, building the Land Rovers and Range Rovers that set the standard for high-performance SUVs and wagons. The 1994 Discovery was its new midsize four-door 4WD wagon, a more modest version of the full-size Rover. The 1995 Defender two-door 4WD utility vehicle was still more rugged, while maintaining consistently high quality. King of the hill, and perhaps of the full-sized 4X4 class, was the Range Rover, whose 1996 edition added new muscle, new front wheels and tires, and a spiffy chrome exhaust system. The standard engine was a 4.0-liter V-8, with a 4.6-liter engine option.

The 1993 Range Rover, a leader in the full-sized luxury SUV class, is powered by a muscular 3.9-liter V-8 engine.

With its aero-styled body, five-spoke alloy wheels, roomy interior, and rugged roadability, the 1994 LRD Discovery is at home in the country and at the country club.

The LR Discovery is the more modestly priced Rover, compared to the high-line Range Rover. This 1992 Discovery demonstrates why the model is a potential contender in the midsize, four-door 4WD wagon category.

Don't let those good looks fool you, the LR Discovery is as tough as they come, as shown by its selection as the official vehicle of the grueling Camel Trophy off-road race since 1989.

Toyota's 1993 Land Cruiser DJ model was that company's entry in the top-of-the-line full-size class. The four-door 4WD wagon had a new 4.5-liter engine, a double-overhead-cam, 24-valve in-line-six engine with 212 bhp. Air-conditioning and cruise control were standard. The 1994 midsize 4Runner SR5 had a V-6 engine and anti-lock braking. The next year the Land Cruiser bowed with a new grille and instrument panel, followed by the debut of the new compact 1996 RAV4.

RAV4 meant Recreational Active Vehicle with 4WD. It was a mini-SUV, based on an existing car platform, and could be considered one of the recent and growing class of hybrid car/SUVs. The 1996 4Runner got pumped with a potent new package, including a brawnier V-6 engine and a muscularly styled exterior that made it one of the most power-ful of its class of midsize SUVs. In 1997 Land Cruiser celebrated its fortieth anniversary with a special edition trim package.

A hybrid vehicle of note was the Subaru 1995 Legacy Outback 4WD compact wagon, debuting with a 2.2-liter four-cylinder engine with 135 bhp. The 1997 Outback would expand on that with a 2.5-liter engine and all-wheel drive (AWD), which directs continuous power to all four wheels at once, allowing maximum grip in all driving situations.

The midsize Nissan Pathfinder moved upmarket with the 1994 LE model for the luxury crowd. The SE model got new alloy wheels and sunroof, and all models had a new instru-ment panel. The 1996 Pathfinder was a new-look makeover model. Mitsubishi Montero used its 1994 model as an entrée into the full-size luxury class SUV line, dropping its entry-level edition and keeping LS and sporty SR packages, both with V-6 engines. The company crashed the midsize market with its new 1997 Montero Sport, basically a chopped-down Montero platform, but lighter and more nimble. Still climbing, the full-size Montero went even more upscale that year, losing the LS manual transmission model, and powering up the V-6 under its hood.

Suzuki meanwhile bid farewell to its controversial Samurai SUV in model year 1995, while giving the surviving Sidekick a new top. The following year found Sidekick with a

Keeping cool is easy for the 1995
Toyota Land Cruiser with its
4.5-liter 212-bhp, in-line-six engine,
and its newly designed dashboard
and revised grille. Air conditioning
is standard, not that it's needed here.

The long-lived Toyota Land
Cruiser reaches its fifth generation with the 1998 model, fea-
turing the company's first-ever
V-8, a 4.7-liter 230-bhp engine. The
model also serves as the platform
for Lexus' luxury LX 470 SUV.

new makeover, sporting a re-styled body and a new 16-valve, 95-bhp engine. The jaunty new Sport package featured a twin cam motor, wider track, and a chrome grille.

Like Sidekick, the Chevy Geo Tracker was a mini-SUV with a truck-style body/chassis construction. Tracker kept pace with its new 1996 four-door model, given a design overhaul from stem to stern, including four-wheel anti-lock brakes. Another late entry in the mini-use mart was Honda's CR-V. This comfortable, Runabout Vehicle (CR-V) was a car/SUV hybrid, similar to RAV4.

The 4WD CR-V was made with birdcage-style unibody construction, and had a four-cylinder engine. Honda's midsize 4X4 was the Passport, which was basically an Isuzu Rodeo platform.

Models multiplied in mid-decade, expanding to fill all niches: The 1996 Lexus LX 450 was an even fancier version of Toyota's Land Cruiser; Acura's 1996 SLX four-door 4WD wagon was a more luxurious Isuzu Trooper; the 1997 Infiniti QX4 took off from a Nissan Pathfinder platform; the 1996 Oldsmobile Bravada was a more luxe version of Jimmy and Blazer; and the 1997 all-new Mercury Mountaineer was targeted at the luxury fanciers in the Explorer class.

And why not? SUVs were in demand as never before. During the eighties, the small car had been the thing. By the mid-nineties, SUV sales were cutting in on small car sales. Mini-van sales were also trending down, as the mid- and full-size SUVs grew at their expense. As the decade nears its close, the SUV has become the thing to beat.

4X4s Forever

By the late nineties, the SUV marketplace had become the arena for hotly contested automotive dominance. One of the most pitched battles was fought in the compact/mini-SUV field.

Perhaps mindful of the mounting popularity of the compacts, Chevrolet's Geo Tracker became the 1998 Chevy Tracker. Available as a two-door convertible or four-door hardtop, Tracker was powered by a standard 1.61-liter four-cylinder engine, and offered optional part-time 4WD. The same year's midsize Blazer had a standard 4.3-liter Vortec V-6 with 190 bhp, while the full-size Tahoe's standard mill was a 5.7-liter V-8 with 255 bhp for real power and towing ability. Insta-Trac part-time 4WD was standard for Tahoe, with optional Auto-Trac full-time 4wd.

The 1998 Toyota 4Runner midsize model has four doors and seats five. Powered by a standard 2.7-liter 150-bhp four-cylinder engine, the well-regarded machine sold 100,000 units the previous year.

The 1998 Chevy
Tahoe 4X4 is fitted
with a standard
Insta-Trac part-
time 4WD system,
with an optional
Auto-Trac full-
time system. The
full-size machine
is market posi-
tioned between the
Suburban and the
midsize Blazer.

Dodge's highly
anticipated re-entry
into the SUV market
is the 1998 Dodge
Durango, based on
the Dakota light-
truck platform.
With a standard
3.9-liter V-6 175-bph
engine, and two
optional V-8s, it's
proved to be a sales
winner straight out
of the starting gate.

GMC's midsize 1998 Jimmy received a sporty new makeover, including a new front end and rear bumper and a standard 4.3-liter V-6 engine, available in two- and four-door versions. A companion vehicle, the 1999 GMC Envoy, is the deluxe edition of the Jimmy, fully loaded with every option and feature that luxury lovers could want. GMC's full-size Yukon SUV remained one of the top in its class, with a standard GM Vortec V-8 engine. Top of the Yukon package line was the Denali SUV, with an overhead-cam 255-bhp V-8. The 1998 model year offered the optional GM OnStar computerized locator system, a sign of things to come.

GMC's high-line, full-size 1998 Yukon's standard 5.7-liter Vortec V-8, 255-bhp engine has real towing power. Prestige options include selectable push-button Autotrac full- time 4WD.

The 1998 Yukon Denali is available with GM's OnStar satellite uplink locator system, making getting lost a thing of the past.

Since making its debut in model year 1995, the Chevy Tahoe has garnered a reputation as a serious SUV with strong towing and workhorse capabilities. The 1998 Tahoe's standard engine is a 5.7-liter mill with 255 bph. Also available is a 6.5- liter Turbo Diesel V-8.

Behold the 1998 Ford Explorer, with its standard 4.0-liter V-6 160-bhp engine. The four-door offers an optional 5.0-liter, 215-bhp V-8 with a permanent 4WD system.

Ford's midsize Explorer remains a phenomenal success story, the best-selling SUV in the United States. The 1998 model had a standard 4.0-liter V-6 with 160 bhp and an optional V-8. A Control Trac full-time 4WD system was available for the V-6 editions, and a permanent no-driver-input 4WD system was a V-8 edition option. Up where the big boys play, in the full-size class, the Expedition pitted itself against the Chevy Suburban and others of its ilk, packing a 4.6-liter standard V-6 and optional V-8 and offering push-button 4WD.

One of the founders of the SUV field, Jeep occupies an enviable position as the twenty-first century closes in. Jeep Wrangler was one of the kings of the compacts, with a standard 2.5-liter four-cylinder engine with 120 bhp and an optional 4.0-liter in-line-six. The midsize Grand Cherokee combined V-8 power with luxury-class accommodations. New for 1998 was the Grand Cherokee premium Limited with a 5.9-liter 245-bhp V-8, one of the most muscular SUV packages available anywhere. Cherokee continued to offer solid, no-frills 4WD motoring with a standard four-cylinder and optional in-line-six.

In a class by itself in SUV excellence and in price was AM General's Hummer, available in two GM V-8 engine options, as a two-passenger and four-passenger hardtop and as a four-door wagon. Another of the stalwarts, Britain's Rover company, celebrated its fortieth anniversary in 1998, continuing the tradition with its workhorse Defender (even a workhorse Rover is a thoroughbred), the midsize Discovery, and the sublime full-size Range Rover.

The 1998 LR Discovery comes in LE and LSE trim packages, both fitted with V-8 engines, including the all aluminum 4.0-liter V-8 with 182 basic horsepower.

Jeep Wrang-
ler now finds
itself compet-
ing with such
compact SUV
contenders
as the Honda
CR-V and
Toyota RAV-4.
The 1996 two-
door four-
seater show-
cases luxe-de-
tailed interior
styling.

Inside and
out, the 1996
Wrangler was
a makeover
model. The
top-of-the-line
engine was a
4.0 in-line-six.

The 1996 Wrangler's new Quadra-Coil suspension and classic truck-type chassis keeps true to the line's tradition of rugged off-roading capability.

FOLLOWING PAGE:
The 1997 Mercedes-Benz ML320 is powered by a 3.2-liter 315-bhp, V-6 engine with automatic transmission, and has full-time 4WD. A V-8 option is due in 1999.

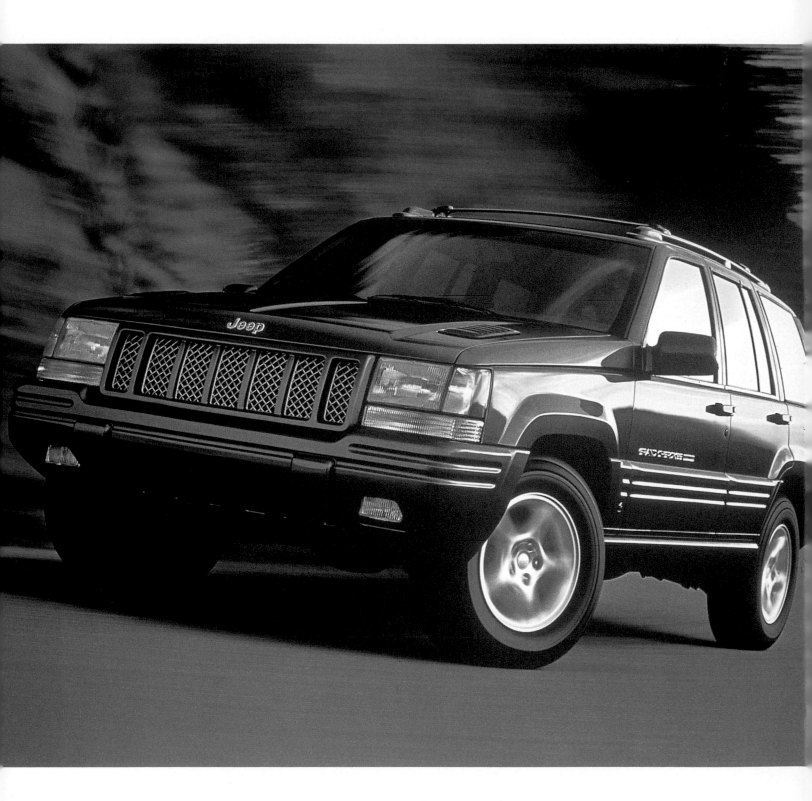

Make way for the muscle SUV, "the fastest Jeep ever," the 1998 Grand Cherokee premium 5.9 Limited, empowering the midsize sportwagon with a burly V-8 engine.

The 1998 Grand Cherokee 5.9 Limited is positioned squarely in the luxury-utility market. Its Quadra-Trac option offers full time 4WD, no driver input necessary.

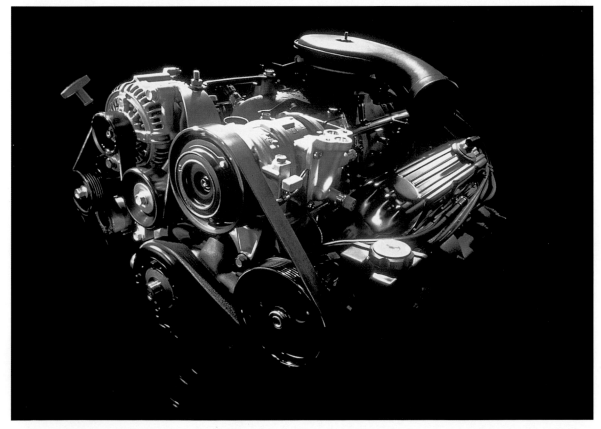

The heart of the 1998 Cherokee Limited: a 5.9-liter V-8 power plant, with 245 basic horsepower.

The 1998 Toyota RAV-4 has a standard 2.0-liter 127-bhp four-cylinder engine with a five-speed manual transmission. New for '98, a softtop convertible.

Car/SUV hybrids continue to gather momentum and popularity. Toyota's RAV4 mini-SUV was built on the Celica car platform, Subaru's four-door Forester with a four-cylinder engine was platformed on the Subaru Impreza-class cars, and Subaru's Legacy Outback was one of the original hybrids. It's certain that such "crossover" vehicles will continue to increase in range and variety in the near future.

At the other end of the spectrum, Ford made ready to release its 1999 mega-SUV, as yet unnamed. Based on the F-350 Super Duty truck platform, the new model will be the biggest yet SUV. Ford's current largest SUV is the new 1998 Lincoln Navigator, Lincoln's first-ever SUV, but the unnamed newcomer

Toyota's RAV-4 has been a compact SUV contender since its 1996 launch. Based on a car platform similar to the Honda CR-V, it offers two- and four-door versions. Shown here is the 1998 model.

The 1998 Lincoln Navigator, the prestigious luxury automaker's first SUV, is a sign of the times. Built on an Expedition platform, this chrome-fronted four-door seats eight and can tow an 8,000 pound (3,600 kilogram) load.

will top even that. With luxury car maker par excellence Lincoln entering the field, along with precision-engineering potentate Mercedes Benz offering its own new ML 320 midsize luxe SUV, it's a real-life example of the old showbiz saying, "Everybody's getting into the act!"

We've seen where the SUV has been. But where is it going? The answer is: Everywhere, from the scrappy compacts and minis barreling along the back-trails off-road, to the full-sized SUVs thronging the freeways and country club parking lots.

And it all began with the army jeep. Not bad for an old "motorized mule" war veteran.

The 1997 Mercedes-Benz mid-size luxury SUV lives up to it's maker's description of it as an "all-activity" vehicle." This is the first time that the renowned German automaker's marque has appeared on a 4X4.

Mercedes-Benz debuted its 1997 ML 320, a four-door, 4WD vehicle that handles like a luxury car. It's positioned at the same market niche shared by the LR Discovery, Ford Explorer, and Jeep Grand Cherokee.

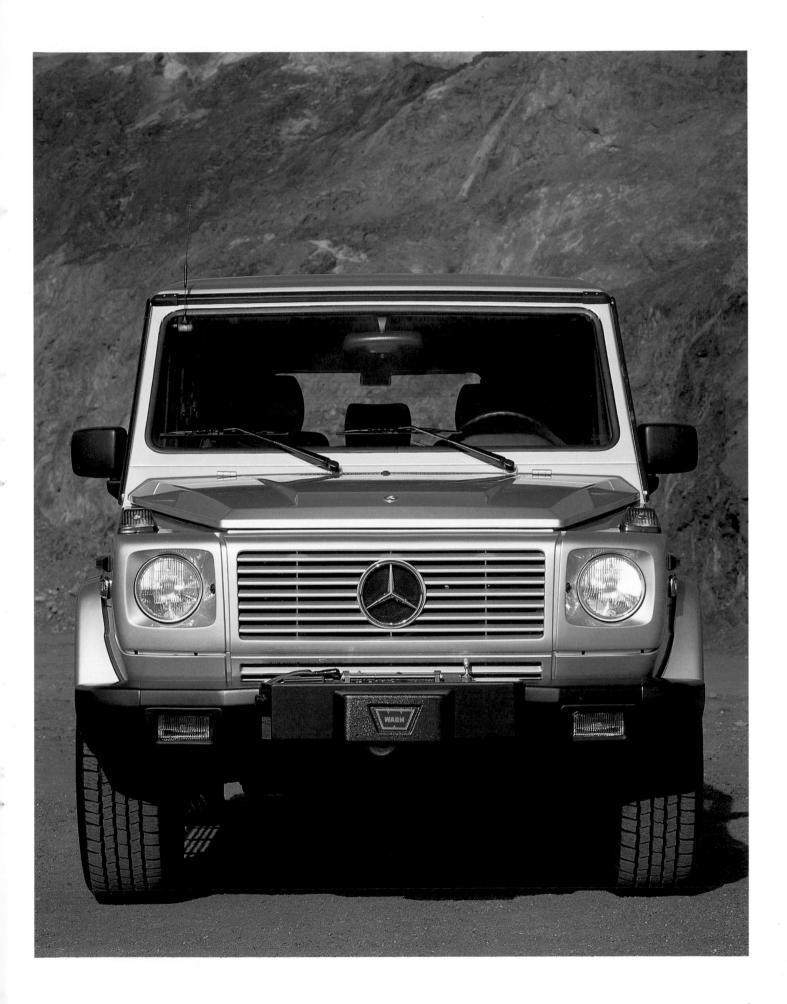

Gardening in Containers

By the Editors of Sunset Books and Sunset Magazine

Lane Publishing Co. • Menlo Park, California

Foreword

Have you noticed how many gardens these days reflect the upsurge in popularity of container gardening? More than ever before, people are discovering this versatile, quite practical way to grow plants. They recognize that with containers, the opportunity to garden reaches everyone—even those limited to raising plants in a window box or on a city rooftop.

At Sunset, our enthusiasm for container gardening goes back many years. In 1952, we published a 64-page, black and white gardening manual called *The Portable Garden*. Since then, we've revised the title, expanded the size, and published three more editions—in 1959, 1967, and now 1977.

Though our editorial approach has changed somewhat from the original edition, our enthusiasm remains the same. We describe the characteristics and growing requirements of over 200 suitable plants and offer dozens of colorful ways to display your favorites, whether you use containers out of necessity or just for pleasure. You'll find helpful ways to feature, mix, match, and move your containers according to the weather, the occasion, or a sudden whim.

Japanese maple (Acer palmatum) *on Sunset patio.*

Supervising Editor: Dorothy Krell

Research and Text: Linda Brandt

Design: Terrence Meagher
Illustrations: E. D. Bills, Terrence Meagher

Cover: Bursting with color are half barrels of yellow and orange marigolds, white marguerites, deep blue lobelia, phlox, petunias, zinnias. Photographed by Don Normark. Design: W. David Poot.

Editor, Sunset Books: David E. Clark

Fifth Printing September 1981

Contents

Special Features

Containers Give Gardening a New Look

Assortment of potted favorites near entry is grouped informally and rotated with the seasons.

Once you've tried growing plants in containers, you will very likely become a devotee of this versatile way of gardening. Whether you tend a few pots of herbs at the kitchen door or landscape your deck completely with tubbed plants, you'll discover that containers make gardening flexible and fun.

Because you can keep plants constantly on the move, container gardening just can't become monotonous. The best each season has to offer can be brought on stage for maximum display, then hidden from sight when its peak show is over. By replacing plants, replanting from one pot to another, or simply rearranging containers, you can refresh your garden in a minor way or give it a complete transformation.

Try plants in pots as seasonal accents, problem solvers, featured displays, or prized collections. They are often utilitarian—a visual or physical barrier, a screen from breezes, a filter for sunshine, even a food garden—and they can work architecturally, either disguising or emphasizing a structural design. They can be an integral part of a formal garden or add a cheerful bit of whimsy to a tiny patio.

If ground space is limited, let containers spill over onto patios, decks, steps, and walkways. If you run out of level space, create a garden in the air by hanging containers from walls, fences, overhangs, or trees, or by training flowering vines up a trellis. And on balconies and rooftops, where ground space is nonexistent, you can depend on containers for a subtle touch of greenery.

Specific suggestions for using container plants follow in this chapter. You'll find numerous landscaping situations that are either enhanced or dependent upon the presence of container plants. The next chapter, "The How-to of Container Gardening," will tell you what you need to know about planting and caring for your plants. And the lists beginning on page 38 describe individual plants especially suited to container life in various situations.

Trio of half barrels *brimming with marigolds and marguerites. Design: W. David Poot.*

Tranquil *garden setting features hydrangea, marguerites, white sweet alyssum.*

Marguerites, *impatiens, begonias, felicias, transplanted from 4-inch pots, were set out just weeks earlier.*

Ideas for display 5

Change your garden with the seasons

One of the most useful roles for container plantings is to bring seasonal change to your garden. With a little know-how for selecting plants, you can keep your garden perky and inviting all year around by rotating containers periodically. While enjoying the flowers of one season, you can prepare for the next one. For example, you can start spring bulbs early in an inconspicuous garden area, then move them to center stage when they're ready to burst into bloom. Later, when flowering is over, you can move them aside to make way for the lively annuals of summer.

Early-blooming shrubs, displayed prominently or set in the background, offer a bit of greenery behind colorful, low-growing flowers. And when your garden begins to suffer from winter doldrums, bring in a tubbed plant with interesting foliage, an unusual shape, or brightly colored berries. An easy solution for a colorless winter garden is ornamental "flowering" cabbages. They thrive in cold weather, and their frilled leaves change colors from shades of pink and rose to purple and lavender.

A favorite garden area gets year-round attention when you span the seasons with flowering plants. One approach is to use a single color theme. For example, yellow calendulas and violas grow in cool months, marigolds in hot summer, and chrysanthemums in autumn.

And what could be more special on holidays and other festive occasions than a color-filled container plant. Here are suggestions to get you started:

- Red, pink, or white begonias in a simple ceramic planter would capture any heart on Valentine's Day. Or, for larger containers, mass 3 or 4 flowering cyclamen in reds, pinks, or white on a green carpet of baby's tears.

- For a fun, but short-lived container plant, consider a *Trifolium repens*—better known as "shamrock." Leaves, divided into 3 leaflets said to be symbolic of the Trinity, have special appeal to many on St. Patrick's Day.

- Fragrant, trumpet-shaped, pure white lilies (*Lilium longiflorum*) are traditional favorites during Easter. Because normal blooming season is midsummer, bulbs must be forced to bloom early.

- For a patriotic salute to the Fourth of July, combine bright red geraniums and blue lobelia. A red, white, and blue hanging basket is easy with three different shades of petunias; or try dwarf scarlet verbena, trailing white sweet alyssum, and blue 'Malibu' petunias.

- Changes to cooler weather mark the beginning of fall color. Yellow, gold, and orange chrysanthemums complement autumn decorations for Halloween and Thanksgiving.

- Christmas marks a special time for container plants— both as gifts and decorations. Traditional red, white, and pink poinsettias and flowering kalanchoes (*Kalanchoe blossfeldiana*) are ever-popular as gifts; so are miniature pines, spruces, and junipers.

- Decorating with red, white, and green can be done in a number of ways: red florists' cyclamen and fluffy white candytuft; pots of red poinsettias stacked on steps to resemble a Christmas tree; a tubbed evergreen brought indoors for a living holiday tree.

Decorate with container plants

Think of container plants as furnishings for your garden or inside your home. You can use them to dramatize an entry, liven up a drab corner, relieve an expanse of paving or bare wall, complement your color scheme, or cover up an empty space.

Here are a few ideas for container plants as decorative elements:

- A container plant offers a friendly welcome when displayed as the focal point of an entry garden.

- Give added interest to an outdoor stairway by placing potted plants at the side of each step.

- Break up the bare sweep of a concrete swimming pool area by creating small flowering clusters with potted plants.

- Make the most of corners. Fill a narrow corner at an entry door with a slim topiary tree. In a more spacious corner, group several containers, varying flower colors or keeping them exactly the same; or display one large container planted with a potpourri of plants.

- Spotlight a bold-leafed plant outside a living-room window for a dramatic nighttime effect.

- If your home is on several levels or you have a balcony, container plants can help improve the view when looking down from the higher level. If neighbors look down on you, hanging plants offer a visual barrier and provide privacy.

- Relieve monotonous expanses of solid brick or masonry with evergreen climbing plants.

- Pots of white-flowering or silvery gray plants such as dusty miller, nicotiana, alyssum, and

(Continued on page 9)

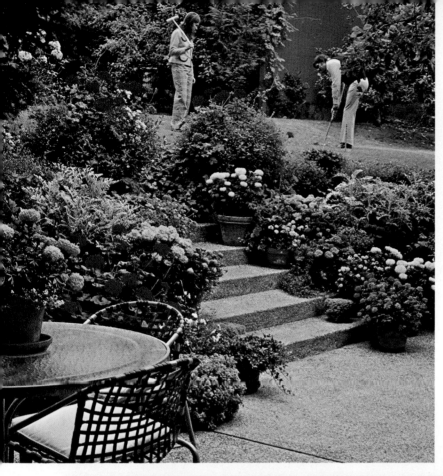

Portable gardens enhance steps and entries

Marigolds, *geraniums, dusty miller, sedum, and ivy flank steps leading from patio to higher garden level. Tiered display offers vivid colors, lush foliage. Design: R. David Adams.*

Grouped informally *on patio landing, white marguerites grow in large Spanish pots. Design: W. David Poot.*

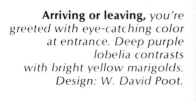

Twin *imported terra cotta pots stationed beside entry hold inviting combination of bright red geraniums, sky blue lobelia. Design: R. David Adams.*

Arriving or leaving, *you're greeted with eye-catching color at entrance. Deep purple lobelia contrasts with bright yellow marigolds. Design: W. David Poot.*

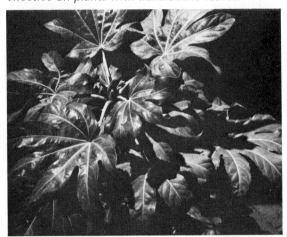

Backlighting *from below is dramatic as well as unique because it seldom occurs in nature. It is effective on plants with translucent leaves.*

Shine a little light on

No matter how colorful the foliage or how unique the branching habits of your most admired container plants, they fade from sight when the sun goes down. But why let them? Instead, give them a chance again, at night— with a little light. Often a single light, positioned in just the right spot, can make all the difference.

When you shine a light on a plant, you create one of five basic effects. To illustrate these effects in their simplest form, we have taken one dramatic plant—the aralia—and lighted it to show you just what can be done.

Take a moment to study the plants in your garden. Think about their overall shape, the containers they're in, and their setting. If you highlighted a few plants, wouldn't your garden take on a totally new dimension?

Shadows *are the striking by-products of lighting here. The shadow on the wall is often more decorative than the plant itself.*

Spotlighting *is selective floodlighting—like shining sunlight through a funnel. Here it dramatizes a cluster of leaves.*

Silhouetting *shows shape and outline, so it is best used with boldly formed plants. Here, panel behind aralia is lighted.*

Floodlighting *is the nearest thing to daylight. It shows the plant much as you see it in the sun, but with a dark background.*

petunias will softly illuminate your garden on dark days and shine out magically on moonlit nights.

• Try window boxes to brighten a view from inside the house. They are perfect for narrow balconies or ledges where other plantings are unsuitable.

• Circle a fountain or birdbath with colorful potted annuals.

• For an eye-catching conversation piece, plant a miniature African violet like 'Dolly Dimple' in a favored china tea cup.

• Plant matching containers with identical flowering plants for a dramatic effect. Locate them on either side of an entrance or walkway.

• An easy, decorative way to show off home-grown herbs is to plant them in flue or sewer tiles or concrete building blocks. Mass them in the corner of a patio or submerge them halfway into the ground.

Bring nature's touch indoors

In the last decade, we've witnessed a growing enthusiasm for raising indoor plants. Besides sensing the intrinsic value, people consider their plants decorative elements that can be used in a number of imaginative ways.

Because clay and plastic pots often lack interest and appear bare, you may choose to mask them with decorative sleeves made of more imaginative materials. Wicker baskets, ceramic and porcelain dishes, and containers of pewter, brass, and other metals offer fancy coverups for dull pots.

Just about any spot lends itself to container plants. You can tuck them in bookshelves, on windowsills, and on countertops; use them singly or in groups in entryways and halls. Suspend them from the ceiling, mass them in corners, or grow them in bottle gardens—even in plain water.

An oddly shaped room—too long, narrow, or high—or one with harsh lines that need disguising can be brought into perspective with the addition of potted plants. It's easy to camouflage an empty corner's bareness by suspending bushy, trailing types (Boston or Roosevelt ferns or grape ivy) over a grouping of upright plants below. Or if your room is quite large, break up the expanse with floor planters positioned across one section.

You'll find an added bonus in rooms that lead into the garden or open onto a patio. Houseplants can bridge the gap between indoors and out, creating a sense of spaciousness and continuity when positioned on both sides of the entryway.

Apartment dwellers can convert a closet into a unique plant display. After removing the door, install a few shelves and mount fluorescent tubing underneath, gaining an ideal place to house a favorite collection of small potted plants.

In summer an empty fireplace becomes a focal point when filled with a few potted plants. Bold-leafed varieties such as schefflera, *Dracaena*, *Dieffenbachia*, and split-leaf philodendron are especially impressive. Or you might want to cover the hearth with a carpet of seasonal color—winter cyclamen in shades of bright pink and red, spring-blooming bulbs in a rainbow of choices, and summer and autumn annuals.

A window-lined garden room is a house plant enthusiast's dream. Ideally, north-facing windows provide good even light throughout the day without the damaging effect caused by harsh, direct sunlight. Windows facing east and west allow intense light (possibly direct sunlight) to filter in during either the morning or afternoon; south-facing windows generally receive the most intense sunlight for the greatest part of the day.

Here's a different idea for displaying house plants: transform a glass-topped coffee table into a showcase for your flowering favorites (African violets, gloxinias, impatiens, cyclamen) by arranging them singly or in groups underneath the glass.

And if you're tired of growing plants potted the traditional way, why not go "dirtless"? Many philodendrons, wandering Jew, English and devil's ivy, and arrowhead vine grow well in containers filled with just water.

Plant winning combinations

Most plants are by their very nature beautiful, but when grouped in a single container, they can lose some appeal. Picking harmonious combinations isn't always easy. Some typical problems: choosing too many colors or putting the wrong colors together; selecting plants that reach maturity and bloom at different times; and combining plants that require different amounts of sun, moisture, and food.

The suggestions below should give you ideas for successful combinations. Besides being attractive, our combinations create environments where the individual plants thrive and complement each other.

Here are some winning combinations:

• For a lush arrangement in a shady spot, fill a hanging basket with begonias, primroses, and asparagus or pellaea ferns.

• Late-blooming, lemon yellow, miniature

Red *and white petunias, blue lobelia brighten fence; pots drop into holes sawed in redwood brackets.*

Brightly colored *mixed bouquets in wire-frame half baskets dot natural redwood fence. For profuse bloom, water and feed well.*

White and lavender *fairy primroses, fuchsias along redwood fence create living fresco.*

Plants dress up fences, posts, and windows

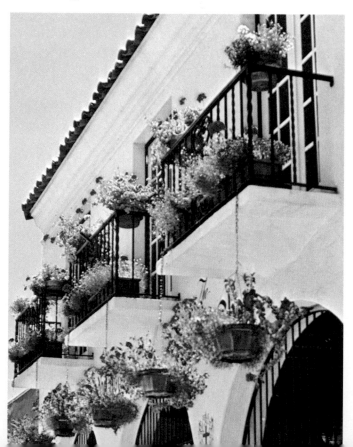

Leafy asparagus ferns *hang from balcony supports. Planter boxes, stained to match house siding, hold pots of purple petunias. Design: W. David Poot.*

Railed balconies *hold planter boxes, mounted clay pots of lobelia, geraniums. Redwood planters hang from heavy chains.*

daffodils and golden brodiaea are especially appealing under an autumn flowering cherry.
• In mild spring climates, fairy primrose combines well with tulips, hyacinths, and other bulbs.
• Edge a vegetable-filled half barrel with low-growing annuals—sweet alyssum, dwarf marigolds, petunias, lobelia, violas.
• Fill a long planter box within arm's reach of the kitchen door with five popular herbs—rosemary, chives, mint, parsley, and tarragon.
• Cloverlike oxalis covers a moss-lined wire basket; let begonias or impatiens peek out—choose shades of pink, red, or orange.
• Chinese hibiscus, a showy shrub with exotic, colorful flowers, grows above a pure white, low-growing carpet of sweet alyssum.
• In a sunny location, set large pots of yellow trumpet daffodils in a sea of baby-blue-eyes or blue forget-me-nots.
• Brightly colored, solid, or patterned containers are often hard to plant. Tone down the overall look by selecting gray-hued plants like silvery yarrow, stonecrop (*Sedum spathulifolium*), or Jerusalem sage to blend with other plants in the container.
• At the base of a tubbed pink flowering almond, plant white, pink, or blue dwarf hyacinths.
• Include a spidery group of succulents in a hanging pot. Sedums with trailing stems and ice plant with pointed leaves make an excellent choice for container gardens in hot desert areas.
• Brightly colored sparaxis combined with silvery gray *Sedum spathulifolium* create an exciting twosome in a low clay container.
• The humid atmosphere of terrariums and bottle gardens is ideal for these plants in any combination: miniature palms, ivies, philodendrons, peperomias, aralia.

Display your favorites

If your container plants have a special feature, give them a chance to perform.

Whether your favorites are a variety of popular geraniums or a rare collection of succulents, give them a starring role. Place them where everyone who passes can appreciate them; but most of all, make sure that you yourself will enjoy them many times during the day. Tubbed daphne, for example, can be placed near an entry or an open window so its fragrance and flowers can be enjoyed throughout the blooming season.

Why not set aside a special display area for your bonsai or succulent collection, or display a special plant on a pedestal as you would a piece of sculpture? If your favorite plant has unusual form or foliage, set it off dramatically against a plain wall. You can easily transform a monotonous fence into a showplace for a collection of hanging fuchsias.

Or perhaps your favorites simply consist of small potted herbs or a few treasured seedlings rooting in sand. A well-exposed kitchen window or shelf often can be converted into a miniature greenhouse, providing your plants with protection during their earliest growth period.

Rough terra cotta pots, interesting rocks, driftwood, even a scooped-out log make perfect natural settings for ferns and cacti. A collection of succulents is easily displayed in a single container when you fill each cup of a strawberry jar with a different species. If you enjoy the delicate look of miniature roses, transplant 2 or 3 plants from 4-inch pots into a 10-inch container. You create a rounded mass of tiny, colorful blooms.

You might display your favorites in the same way you would a prized collection—under glass. Open and glass-covered terrariums offer the perfect climate for many indoor favorites; most nurseries and garden centers have suitable small plants in 2-inch pots. And when you plant a garden in a glass container, you transform an ordinary brandy snifter, fishbowl, wine or water bottle (clear, not colored), or aquarium tank into a miniature tropical isle.

Experiment—the results may surprise you

Container gardening gives you an opportunity to try new plants, one at a time or in groups. If you decide that you don't like a plant, or if it doesn't perform well for you, you can move it away without leaving a gaping hole in your garden.

Experiment with the plants you already have. Almost any plant can be grown, at least for a time, in a container. A plant that goes unnoticed when massed in the garden with others may take on an exciting new personality when isolated in a container. Black bamboo, for example, can divide and delicately screen off a patio area when potted in a large tub; or if rotated indoors, it can separate a living room from an entry hall.

And if you have a plant that is ailing or rarely shows signs of growth, simply potting it up and moving it to a new location may bring it back to health.

Experiment, too, with the containers you choose. You don't have to limit yourself to nurseries and garden centers. Look in antique and import stores or visit a local building supply yard.

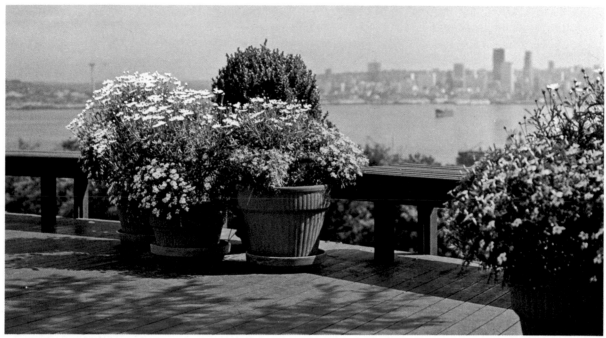

Panoramic *city skyline makes impressive background for container plants. Throughout year, deck features wide variety of plants, all in containers. Design: W. David Poot*

Decks and rooftops depend on containers

Vivid colors *of marigolds, geraniums surround deck. Design: Michael Westgard.*

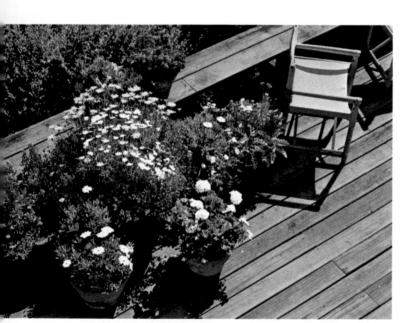

View from top floor *reveals deck brimming with colorful potted annuals. Containers can be moved about, replanted throughout season. Design: R. David Adams.*

Formal rooftop garden *features containers of trimmed boxwood; privet trained into standards; red, white, blue-flowering combinations of petunia, alyssum, lobelia. Planter boxes mounted on casters allow easy rearranging.*

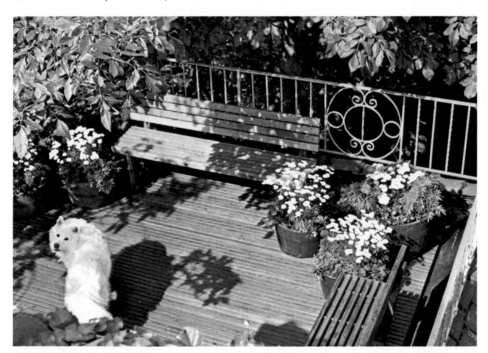

Garage rooftop,
*resurfaced and enclosed
with iron railings,
features matching barrels
of marguerites, marigolds.
Design: W. David Poot.*

Use your imagination and seek out the unusual. Sometimes the most unlikely objects make exciting plant containers.

Fill an old washtub with colorful annuals or float water lilies (or other bog and aquatic plants) in a wide-mouthed clay jar. Or comb through the kitchen for possible containers—teakettles, copper pots and pans, soup tureens, casserole dishes. House plants with interesting foliage look particularly attractive in them; so do showy spring bulbs.

And what child isn't fascinated by the sight of germinating seeds? Place a few bean seeds in a glass jar filled with damp cotton. Or fill a shallow container with damp cheesecloth and sprinkle with alfalfa or cress seeds. In a matter of days you'll have grown delicious sprouts.

Solve your landscaping problems

Many times a container planting becomes that extra "something" needed to solve the trickiest landscaping problem. Tall, sturdy plants grown in large tubs or half barrels become barriers, screening out an unattractive view, acting as a wind protector, or providing privacy from the rest of the garden. They can direct traffic through an entryway or patio, serve as buffers for cars parked in a driveway, or soften the harsh line of a new wall.

Narrow side yards often present a problem—too small for a patio, yet awkward for big planting beds. But a few well-placed containers, on the ground or hanging from a fence, fill the empty spaces effectively. And to increase privacy and break up the horizontal line, space pots of flowering plants along the top of a low wall.

Berry-producing bushes like *Mahonia* and *Pyracantha* give a much needed lift to drab, light-toned walls. Or perhaps you want to cover a wall with fast-growing vines. Many grow from seed to maturity in a hurry and produce a spectacular effect by covering large areas in a mere 6 to 8 weeks.

Tubbed vines are useful near windows, too. They can shade rooms on a hot afternoon during the summer, yet leave the area open for sun during the winter. A leafy, green curtain—actually pots of scarlet runner beans trained on nylon string— brings a unique, natural look to a viewless kitchen window (see page 76).

Some of the most popular and useful vines to help solve landscaping problems are sweet pea, morning glory, scarlet runner bean, trailing types of nasturtiums, and cardinal climber.

Gardeners who live in mobile homes or condominiums find that containers make a garden possible where one would not otherwise survive. In areas where soil is poor, drainage is bad, ground rodents persist, or weather conditions are extreme, container plantings are a perfect solution.

In dry, paved areas, try sinking pots of wind-resistant succulents or woody shrubs into a bed of gravel. If your garden is sunny, you may be able to grow shade-loving plants in a breezeway or shaded entry; if you have too much shade, garden in tubs, boxes, or large pots wherever you find a bit of sunshine. And if the possibility of frost or snow threatens in your area, you can just move your containers to a protected spot or a well-lighted room indoors.

Large city lots and country places often have corners or areas that are difficult to water. What you need in these places are durable plants in containers that manage with minimum watering or seasonal rainfall, and perhaps thrive in full sun.

Set the stage for entertaining

Flowers have always played an important part in entertaining; no party seems quite complete without them. So why not try working container plants into your next indoor or outdoor party theme?

Many outdoor plants lend themselves to indoor party situations. To some you may wish to add a bit of foolishness or whimsy, and to others, lights or candles. Some may look festive with no decoration at all.

Here are a few ideas for creating special party effects with container plants:

• Welcome your guests as they arrive by massing containers of colorful blooms at the entry or arranging them to flank a walk or driveway.

• If you have a leafless shrub with a dramatic form, drape it with sparkling lights and place it where it will brighten a dark garden corner.

• Use container plantings to demarcate special garden party areas: barbecue, beverage table, dance floor, games.

• Hang large ornaments—balloons, big paper flowers, or lanterns—from tubbed trees or from a plant trained into a sturdy standard. For an evening party, illuminate the entire container from below.

• Display container plants as table centerpieces or buffet decorations.

• Add twinkling enchantment indoors by stringing tiny Christmas tree lights in palms or other tall house plants.

Natural redwood barrier *with built-in planters prevents unwanted traffic across lawn. Both moss-lined baskets and planter boxes contain Cascade petunias.*

Massed *with long-stemmed marguerites, Spanish pots line patio edge and visually separate garden levels. Design: W. David Poot.*

Container plants become barriers and screens

Carefully positioned *tubbed bamboo screens view into patio, protects area from harsh sun, drying winds.*

One-of-a-kind containers

Hollowed-out birch log *rests securely in niches carved from two smaller logs, holds red fibrous begonias.*

Fish poacher *makes splendid container for hyacinths on dining table. Bulbs grow individually in 4-inch pots concealed under sphagnum moss.*

Delicate *maidenhair fern grows in planter pocket surrounded by aquarium. See-through acrylic plastic was used to build unique compartmented planter.*

Violas *slipped into wood splint basket hang near front door. Plants grow in plastic bag filled with soil.*

Spilling *over sides of antique German wine barrel is perennial favorite, ivy geranium.*

Dutch soup tureen *serves as display container for pot of white daffodils.*

Asparagus sprengeri *grows in hollowed-out planting pocket near top of 3-foot driftwood stump.*

The How-to of Container Gardening

Quick color *from lobelia, marguerites, fibrous begonias, impatiens, felicias, marigolds.*

In this section we describe the fundamentals of container gardening. You'll find information on possible container choices, planting techniques, potting mixes (both prepackaged and ones to make yourself), and the basics for plant upkeep—watering, feeding, pruning, dealing with pests and diseases, and providing weather protection.

You'll also find directions for planting a moss-lined basket, step-by-step instructions for building some containers, and tips for moving large, heavy containers easily.

Containers are half the picture

Pots, boxes, half-barrels, baskets—by definition, anything that holds soil in which a plant will grow can be a container. But the function of a container is really twofold. Not only does it hold a plant and its root system together, a container also complements the plant with its color, texture, shape, and size.

When selecting a container, keep in mind just how you are going to use it. Should it be lightweight, nonporous, made out of clay, portable? Perhaps large and decorative, or delicately simple? Should you buy one or build one, or do you already have one—what about that discarded washtub in the back of the garage?

As you can see, your choices are endless.

Here are three points to consider when selecting a container:

● **Porosity.** Containers fall into two categories: porous and nonporous. Porous containers are those made of materials that water and air penetrate, such as pots made of unglazed clay and pressed pulp, boxes of untreated wood, and moss-lined baskets. Nonporous containers—glazed, plastic, or metal pots and some treated or lined wooden boxes, for example—prevent air and moisture from penetrating.

Soil in porous containers dries out more quickly, so you'll need to water more frequently. On the other hand, to prevent roots in nonporous containers from becoming waterlogged, you must provide the best possible drainage and soil aeration.

● **Size.** A good rule for deciding appropriate container size is to get something an inch or two larger in diameter than the plant's nursery container. If you are starting with young seedlings that haven't yet really begun to grow, or for baskets lined with moss, allow an additional 2 to 3 inches across.

For a plant in a 1-gallon can, use an 8 or 9-inch pot or a 14-inch basket. Use a 12 to 14-inch pot or a 16-inch basket for a planting that involves two or three 1-gallon plants or for a plant contained in a 5-gallon can.

Remember that a 12-inch container filled with soil may weigh 30 pounds or more, and a 16-inch one up to 60 pounds. This is something to consider if you are thinking of hanging your plant from a patio overhang.

● **Drainage.** Poor drainage is a notorious cause of failure in container gardening. The planting mix must be sufficiently porous for water to drain readily, yet contain enough organic matter to keep the root area moist between waterings. If water collects at the bottom of the container instead of being absorbed by the soil, however, it can rot the roots and drown the plant. The best solution is a hole in the bottom to allow excess water to run out.

If you've found the perfect container, but it has no hole, turn the pot upside down and drill one yourself. For an average size container (about 8 to 12 inches in diameter) one ½-inch hole is sufficient. Use an electric or hand drill for wooden boxes and plastic pots. For clay and ceramic pots, use an electric drill with masonry or carbide bits. To prevent cracking, support the pot on a sturdy block of wood; drill with a small bit first and then increase the bit size until you reach the desired hole diameter. You can also make drilling easier by adding a little water from time to time.

Feet on clay pots and cleats under wood boxes allow water to drain freely; this prevents decay in some woods.

For indoor containers and for outdoor ones that might stain patios or decks, it is a good idea to use saucers or trays. You can prevent seepage through saucers of clay or other porous materials by coating the inside with an asphalt or other waterproof paint.

Clay pots: the near-perfect container

Undoubtedly the most familiar container is the red terra cotta or clay pot. Its natural unglazed appearance enhances any plant, indoors or out. Versatile terra cotta, available in a wide variety of sizes and shapes, looks attractive in most situations and on most finished surfaces. Some nurseries and garden centers also carry clay pots in earthy tones such as tan, cream, black, and chocolate brown (the color used for classical bonsai specimens). The only disadvantages to unglazed pots seem to be that they are breakable and tend to dry out rapidly in warm weather.

Glazed clay pots, more decorative in texture and color than the unglazed types, are especially well suited for indoor or patio use. The glaze produces a nonporous finish—white, black, or practically any color—that prevents moisture from evaporating and thus cuts down on watering. You

Redwood tubs

Hanging redwood planter

Hanging wire basket

Half-basket wire frame

Strawberry pot

Venetian pot

Spanish pot

Paper pulp pot

Redwood boxes

Redwood planter with plastic liner

Glazed pot

This collection of containers is just a sampling of the many types available.

can liven up any plant with a colorful glazed pot; just be sure to select a color that complements the foliage and flowers rather than detracting from them.

Although proportions may differ slightly among pots by various manufacturers, standard clay pots are classified and sold by their diameter. Many of the more ornate ones—Spanish and Venetian pots, strawberry planters, and wide-mouthed lemon jars—are decorative versions of the basic terra cotta pot. We have listed the most useful and popular kinds below.

● **Standard.** Utilitarian rather than beautiful, these pots are at least as tall as they are wide across the top, and frequently taller. Available in 2-inch to 16-inch sizes, they have wide, heavy rims. They come with either predrilled or knock-out drainage holes. The greater depth provides more space for roots, but these pots often seem too tall for the plants in them.

● **Standard fern pot** (also called azalea pot or ¾ pot). Three-quarters as high as wide, these pots are in better proportion to most plants than

regular standards. Available in 4-inch to 14-inch sizes, they are excellent for plants with shallow roots, such as azaleas and ferns.

● **Venetian pots.** Symmetrical and somewhat formal, Venetian pots are available in 7½-inch to 20-inch sizes. Their sides curve slightly inward at the top; a design of concentric bands is impressed into the clay.

● **Spanish pots.** These graceful pots have outward-sloping sides and flaring lips. Available in 8-inch to 12-inch sizes. Spanish fern pots in 12 to 18-inch sizes are also available.

● **Saucers, pans.** Bulb or seed pans vary slightly, but they are typically less than half as high as wide. Resembling deep saucers with drainage holes, they are available in 6-inch to 12-inch sizes.

● **Bowls, jars.** Bowl-like planters—some shallow, wide, and round-bottomed; some with feet; others with flaring sides—are available in various sizes. The pocketed strawberry jar with cups for soil on its sides and the Mexican olla are two favorites.

Hanging clay pot

Hanging redwood planter

Soy tubs

Concrete pot

Standard fern pot

Standard clay pot

Redwood planter box

Flare-sided redwood planter

Three-legged pot

Bonsai pot

Half-barrel

Plastic pot

Also popular are textured concrete and aggregate containers. They're available in varied styles, but most are large and quite heavy when filled with soil. You may have to drill drainage holes in some. (See page 19.)

Tubs, boxes, barrels—the wood way

Offering a natural, usually informal setting for plants are wooden tubs, boxes, and half-barrels. All are well suited for housing most plants— colorful annuals planted in a mixed bouquet to good-sized shrubs and trees.

Roughly defined, the difference between a box and a tub is shape. A box is typically square; a tub has a circular or hexagonal base, with sides constructed of staves held in place by hoops. Barrel halves and soy tubs fit this description; however, large round ceramic containers are often referred to as tubs, too.

Good wooden containers should be decay-resistant and retain moisture. They should also be thick enough that heat, even from the hot summer sun, will penetrate slowly and not dry

roots too quickly. Durable woods such as redwood, oak, and cedar are widely used for container construction. Though these containers require no preservative treatment, you can coat the inside with a nontoxic preservative (avoid creosote), or use a liner made of plastic with holes punched in the bottom.

To prevent excessive loss of moisture, check that joints fit tightly. The bottom of the tub should be raised an inch or more with legs, blocks, or cleats. If necessary, you can usually drill drainage holes in the base.

The expected shape of your plant at maturity is a good guide for determining the shape of your container; just be sure there is ample depth to allow for root growth. For example, a square box is appropriate for a low, bushy azalea or gardenia; a tall tub fits a tapering false cypress or boxwood; and a half-barrel is suitable for growing vegetables and annuals.

One further consideration—weight. Because a cubic foot of soil weighs from 50 to 90 pounds, moving wooden containers can be a *real* problem. (See page 33 for ways to move large containers.)

Halves of barrels originally built to hold liquids are better for containers than others because they have thicker walls and are less apt to leak. Coating the inside with wood preservative and the hoops with rust deterrent will lengthen a barrel's lifetime.

Window boxes—either manufactured or built at home—are often quite heavy. Dependable supports (lag screws or bolts) are therefore necessary to secure them properly to the house studs enclosing the window. For extra security, position the box so it tips slightly back toward the house.

If you build your own, use lumber at least 1 inch thick to prevent the box from warping. Caulk seams so draining water won't stain the house. Width and length measurements will vary, but remember that a depth of at least 9 inches is essential for active plant roots.

Paper pots—the latest wrinkle

Pulp pots, made of compressed, recycled paper, have many advantages. They are comparatively inexpensive and lightweight. Depending on how wet their surfaces are, tubs vary in color from a sun-bleached gray to a water-soaked brownish black. Most people find them attractive or at least easy to tolerate.

Good-sized pulp pots, 18 inches in diameter and 12 inches deep, are excellent for vegetables, herbs, and showy annuals. Since they are easier to carry than other containers of the same size, empty or full, they are particularly suited to decks, rooftops, and other places where you must hand-carry everything. When kept on surfaces other than soil, pulp pots last about 3 years, possibly more.

Containers to look up to

What could be more striking than a beautiful flowering plant suspended right before your eyes?

Near windows and doorways, on fence posts and walls, from wood beams and overhangs, even from trees—the most unlikely spots can be filled instantly with foliage and flowers. Just make sure to find a support that can bear the weight of your container, its soil and water, and the plants.

Popular hanging containers include clay, plastic, and ceramic pots, redwood and cedar boxes, and wire baskets lined with moss. In cool-summer climates, plants thrive in any of these containers, but in hot-summer areas, wooden boxes and plastic pots are more suitable because they retain moisture longer.

If you use moss-lined baskets, be aware that they will drain freely from the sides and bottom whenever you water. You may prefer to use them only in the garden and avoid hanging them above any surface that stains easily or can't be cleaned.

Using strong galvanized wire, suspend your containers from substantial lag-thread clothesline hooks or screw eyes. These are strong enough to bear the weight without pulling out.

Plastic is a possibility

It may not look as earthy as clay or wood, but plastic has its place in container gardening. Plastic pots are durable yet lightweight, versatile yet inexpensive, and they are nonporous, so you need to water less often.

A variety of designs in many sizes and colors awaits you. Some have saucers already built on; others have predrilled holes for attaching hangers. Or you may be intrigued by clear plastic pots that show soil and roots.

Many 1-gallon and 5-gallon plants come in plastic nowadays, and some gardeners choose not to transplant at all. They either bury pots directly into the ground (this is especially practical in areas where good soil is not available) or disguise pots by slipping them into larger, more decorative sleeves. If you do choose to transplant, however, just moisten the root mass, turn the container upside down, and tap its rim firmly. Plants slide out easily.

Containers from unlikely objects

As long as adequate drainage is provided, you can use all sorts of unlikely objects to hold plants. Just experiment a little. Flue tiles and other building materials, natural driftwood and old hollowed logs, antique pots—even washtubs and sinks can be converted into unusual containers.

You may also choose to grow plants in regular pots that are disguised by slipping them into a more decorative second home. Fill in the gaps between the two containers with sphagnum moss or damp peat. Also see pages 16–17.

Tips on potting and repotting

Whether you start your own plants from seed or buy nursery stock—seedlings, bedding plants, burlap-wrapped shrubs, or bare root trees—the methods of planting in containers vary. Here are some pointers on planting and transplanting that will help you get off to a good start.

Getting ready

Before you plant in a used pot or box, take the trouble to scrub it well with hot water and a

If roots *of young plant show through or twine around outside of root ball, gently loosen them before transplanting.*

Plants *usually are repotted into containers one size larger. Shave root ball, making ¼-inch cuts. Place in larger pot, firming in new soil around edges.*

Here are two ways *to remove stubborn plants from large containers. Let soil dry slightly; root ball shrinks and slides out easily when container rim (protected with cloth) is tapped with mallet. Or try floating root ball out of container by forcing water through drain hole.*

brush. This will eliminate any pests and diseases from previous plants and soil. If your container is porous, soak it in water before you plant, so it won't absorb moisture from the potting mix. Otherwise, the root ball will shrink away from the container's sides and water will drain right out.

Cover the drainage hole with a curved shard or with stones or a square of fine-mesh wire screen, to prevent clogging and minimize soil filtering through. For containers without drainage holes, prevent soil from souring by spreading on the bottom a ½ to 1-inch layer of coarse sand mixed with granulated charcoal. (*Note:* Use gardening, not barbecue, charcoal.)

Planting

Wet the soil of each plant before removing it from its nursery container. Not only will this make

removal easier, but the root ball won't break apart or stick to the container.

Some bedding plants are grown in flats or market packs (2 to 12 plants per pack). Remove these in individual soil blocks—as you do brownies from a pan—with a putty knife or spatula. Leave as much soil around the roots of each plant as possible.

Bedding plants in packs of plastic cells (usually six plants per pack) pop out easily when you push the plant up from the bottom of each cell.

To remove a plant from a small pot, invert the pot with one hand and tap it gently against a ledge to loosen the roots. Use the other hand to support the root ball, with the plant stem between your fingers.

Many nurseries now offer 1-gallon size and larger plants in plastic or paper pots, as well as in traditional metal cans. If your plant is in a metal can, use tin snips or a manufactured can cutter to cut the sides apart; your nurseryworker will do this for you if you wish. Then turn the container on its side, loosen the plant, and *gently* pull it out.

Check to see if the roots are tightly compacted around the outside of the root ball (a condition known as "rootbound" or "potbound"). If so, score roots lightly in several places with a sharp knife and loosen them gently with your fingers. This will stimulate new root growth outward into the new soil.

For severely potbound plants whose roots have formed a solid mass, make several cuts from top to bottom down the side of the root ball, running your finger through the cuts to fray the roots if necessary.

You can plant large shrubs and trees, or those balled and burlapped, in paper pots just as you would canned plants—with one exception. For paper pots, first punch a few holes in the sides; then, just before you cover the root ball with soil, cut away the top wrapping that shows above the surface. For balled plants wrapped in burlap, remove the twine and fold back the burlap, but don't remove it from the root ball. Instead, trim off the excess at the top to reduce bulk. Plants are now ready to be covered with soil. Both paper fiber and burlap will decompose in time.

For planting bare root trees, see page 29.

Now pour some moist (not soggy) potting mix into your container. This soil cushion should be deep enough that when you set the plant in the container, the top of its root ball will be about

Soil mixes

Good potting soil combines organic materials (ground bark, peat moss, sawdust, compost, leaf mold) and mineral materials (sand, vermiculite, perlite) in proportions that drain freely, provide ample air for root respiration, and supply nutrients for healthy growth. Some gardeners who do a lot of planting and have adequate storage space prepare their own mix, in a wheelbarrow or on a clean driveway. But for potting a typical number of plants, it is probably less troublesome to buy prepared mix in bags from a nursery or garden center.

What's in premixed potting soil? Usually a wood product such as nitrogen stabilized fir bark or redwood sawdust (the specific product may vary according to locality); sand, vermiculite, or perlite; and fertilizers and lime. With a 2-cubic-foot bag of potting soil you can pot 12 to 15 plants from 1-gallon cans into 10 or 12-inch containers. Or you can fill an entire planter box 36 inches long, 10 inches deep, and 8 inches wide.

If you want to mix your own but don't have a favorite recipe, here's a good basic mix* that yields about 3 cubic feet. It's fine for most outdoor container plants.

2 cubic feet	nitrogen stabilized ground bark, peat moss, or other organic material
1 cubic foot	uniform fine sand or sandy loam
1⅓ cups	0-10-10 or equivalent dry fertilizer
1¾ cups	dolomite limestone

Azaleas, rhododendrons, camellias, and fuchsias prefer a slightly acidic soil mix.* Blend together:

4 or 5 parts	coarse-textured peat moss
1 part	composted leaf mold

Indoor containers, hanging baskets, and outside containers in sheltered areas need a lightweight soil mix.* Blend together:

2 parts	Basic Mix (left)
1 part	vermiculite or perlite

*Because these three mixes contain no nitrogen, they can be stored for as long as 6 months, possibly longer in a dry spot. When it's time to plant, add nitrogen—either in slow-release capsules (tablets) or other forms such as bloodmeal—to guarantee nourishment for proper plant growth..

1 or 2 inches below the rim. Continue filling in with soil, tamping it down lightly with your fingers or a stick.

After planting

Water thoroughly. A good method for small pots is to set them in a pan of water until the soil seems uniformly damp. Water large containers on the soil surface until water drips from the drainage hole. If your pot or box is undrained, apply an amount of water equal to about one-fourth of the total volume of soil in the container.

To help them through the shock of transplanting, set newly potted plants in a shady, protected location for a day or two.

Repotting

After 2 years or more in a container, plants are likely to be rootbound and in need of fresh soil. If roots show through the drainage hole or if, after you've knocked the plant out of its pot, you find roots matted on the outside of the root ball, it's time to repot.

Dump the plant onto a clean surface—a sturdy canvas ground cloth works well. Carefully pull away some of the old potting soil (if any remains) and any other debris. Shave the edges of the root mass and score it with a knife as directed for rootbound plants (see page 23). Scrub old wooden containers or pots with a wire brush and water. Reposition the plant and refill the container with fresh potting mix enriched with a slow-release fertilizer. Water deeply.

It's best to repot during a plant's dormant period, just before it is due to begin active growth again.

Container plant upkeep

Secluded in a damp, woodsy spot, a hardy sword fern survives without the slightest aid from man. But when it is confined in a container, that same fern becomes dependent, relying completely on us to supply its essential needs—water, food, warmth, light, and air.

Once you understand the basics of container culture, keeping plants healthy need not be time-consuming or complicated. Here are some tips. They will help you to tell if your plant is thirsty or needs fertilizer. They also discuss pruning and training, the importance of sunlight and weather protection, and how to deal with the more common pests and diseases that bother container plants.

Watering: how often, how much, how to

Exposure to drying air on all sides (even the bottom, in the case of hanging baskets) is the main reason plants in containers need more water than their counterparts in open ground. But the size and type of container as well as the species of plant also determine specific watering needs. Many plants, including ferns and some annuals, prefer constant moisture throughout the growing season, but cacti and succulents strongly object to such conditions. How, then, do you know when it's time to water?

● **How often.** A few gardeners swear they can tell by the weight of a container whether or not the soil is moist. Others tap the sides of their containers. They say that a *ringing* sound suggests that the container needs water, but a *thud* indicates that damp soil remains. Although these practices may work well for some gardeners, the most accurate method involves inspecting the soil itself.

A good rule is to water as soon as the top inch of soil feels dry when you wiggle your finger in it. There are exceptions to this rule, however, so it's best to get to know the needs of your plants (see pages 38–78). You will probably develop a watering schedule, but be flexible and check your containers periodically, especially during temperature extremes.

On hot, windy days you may need to water more often; in damp, cool weather you need to water very infrequently. During their dormant season, plants need much less water. Don't neglect watering completely during the winter months, however. Pots under eaves and overhangs often suffer because gardeners assume that watering isn't necessary during the rainy season.

● **How much.** Apply water directly into a container (from beneath the foliage with flowering plants), allowing excess to run freely from the drainage hole for at least a minute. If the soil is too dry to absorb water immediately (because the water quickly rushes through between soil particles), don't stop watering until you are sure it has taken in as much moisture as it can hold.

To a container without a drainage hole, apply a volume of water equal to about one-fourth the total volume of soil. This amount of water is enough for the plant's needs but not so much that excess accumulates at the bottom to drown the plant.

● **How to.** Surface watering with a gentle flow from a hose or watering tube is probably the easiest method. (*Caution:* Hot water from a hose

Watering ideas

Nylon cord wicks, *forced up into soil through drainage hole or down through top, absorb water from pan reservoir. Plants receive continuous supply of water, so need less attention.*

In warm weather, *pots dry out less if grouped together and set on gravel bed that's kept constantly moist.*

To conserve *water, set plant inside larger pot, fill space between with damp peat, cover with layer of small pebbles.*

Periodic plunge *into a basin of water guarantees constant moisture through soil. Submerge plant and wait for bubbling to stop.*

Simplify *vacation watering by burying pots up to their rim in large box filled with damp peat moss. Locate in a shady spot.*

Drip irrigation *emits a trickle of water into each pot. From garden hose, water travels through plastic pipe and feeds into spaghetti tubes tucked into foliage.*

that has been lying in the summer sun can wilt or destroy tender plants.)

You can also water pots from below by placing them in a large trough or container partially filled with water. Or you can submerge pots in water and wait until the soil stops bubbling; this indicates that water has taken the place of air.

Fuchsias, ferns, and other plants that enjoy humid surroundings benefit from foliage spraying, especially on hot, windy days.

● **When you are away.** How long can your plants live without you? The answer may be as unpredictable as the weather. So for the container gardener, a vacation—even for just a few days—can be a special worry. To relieve any anxieties on your part, locate a reliable neighbor to plant-sit while you are away. Leave precise instructions on what to water, how much, and when. To make the sitter's job easier, group all containers together in a shady spot and leave a hose with a sprinkler attached nearby.

Or you can prevent pots from drying out quickly by placing them in a trench and filling it with wet sawdust or peat. Some gardeners bury their pots directly in the ground.

Indoor plants will absorb moisture easily when placed on porous bricks (½ to 2 inches thick) in a bathtub or sink half filled with water. Or try watering a number of pots with special nylon wicks now available at many nurseries and garden centers (you can make your own from thin nylon clothesline). Push one end down into the soil 1 or 2 inches, and put the other into a wide, water-filled saucer reservoir (see illustration).

Plant feeding

Container plants absorb most of the nourishment they need from the soil around their roots. Nutrients must be replenished as the plant uses them up. This can be done in various ways; some will be more appropriate than others for your particular plant.

First consider how often you water, because draining water carries out nutrients. Then consider the season. Most plants don't need as much fertilizer during their dormant season; however, in warm sunny weather or during the time of active growth, plants need a stepped-up feeding program.

In commercial fertilizers, three primary ingredients—nitrogen(N), phosphorus (P), and potassium (K)—are listed in ratio form, such as 1-10-10 or 30-10-10. Foliage plants benefit from high nitrogen fertilizers (such as 30-10-10) which encourage growth and help leaves retain good color. In contrast, flowering plants—annuals, perennials, vines, and shrubs—thrive on fertilizers high in phosphorus (such as 15-30-15) which build sturdy root systems and encourage flower production.

Because they require slightly different formulas, roses, citrus, and woody plants such as azaleas, rhododendrons, and camellias should be given special food (often called "citrus food," "rhododendron food," etc.). If you have any doubts, use a complete fertilizer such as fish emulsion (5-1-1) or its equivalent for a balanced diet any plant can have.

Fertilizers can be purchased at most nurseries and garden centers in these forms:

● **Liquid.** Watering with diluted liquid fertilizer is a convenient, fast-acting method of feeding both indoor and outdoor container plants. You can encourage steady growth by giving plants continuous nourishment with light applications twice a month.

● **Dry.** Mixed into the top layer of soil, dry fertilizers act more slowly but last appreciably longer. Just remember to water thoroughly *before and after* fertilizing (if plant has dried out, delay feeding a day or two). By moistening the soil first you minimize the chance of fertilizer burn or damage caused by heavy, infrequent feedings.

● **Time-release capsules.** An easy new method of feeding plants, controlled by moisture in the soil, is by slow-release fertilizer granules buried throughout the potting mix. Nutrients diffuse into the water automatically, but no faster than the roots can absorb them. These plant foods release fertilizer for varying lengths of time; some may last for an entire season, depending on the demands of the plant.

● **Foliage fertilizers.** Because most fertilizers are quite harmful to tender leaves, they should be kept off foliage unless heavily diluted. However, some special foliar sprays, containing vitamins and certain trace elements, are designed to be absorbed directly through the leaves, without causing injury to the plant. This kind of foliage fertilizer is absorbed so readily that it often brings about an overnight recovery for an ailing plant.

Pruning and training

Plants raised within the confines of a tub or pot seldom take on the same character they would if allowed to grow naturally in the garden. Therefore, every potted plant will need pruning at some time, if only to renew its shape and direct its growth.

You may also prune for other important reasons: to increase the yield and quality of flowers or fruit; for a special effect; to give a plant new shape and character, as in training a standard; or to make a miniature out of a larger plant.

● **What to cut off.** Before you start to prune your plant for any reason, you must know about terminal buds—the growing buds at the ends of all branches. These tip buds add length to the branches by drawing energy from the plant during active growth. Therefore, if a terminal bud is cut or pinched back, growth is diverted instead to

Pruning for special effects

'Debutante' camellia *chosen to be trained as standard because of a straight stem, full growth.*

Side shoots *are removed up to 3½ feet above base. Camellia is repotted into decorative clay container.*

Insert stake. *Tie stem in several places below head. Pinch back after bloom for new growth, compactness, more flowers next year.*

Colorado blue spruce, *2½ feet high, just as it came from nursery. First, remove from can, begin thinning twiggy branches to open up top of tree. If necessary, score roots (see page 23), trim to fit container. Set tree in pot, add soil, firm in around roots. Soak pot from below in tub of water, spray top of tree lightly with water to keep it clean and cool.*

other lateral buds. This is an excellent way to direct growth just the way you want it.

A young chrysanthemum, for example, will form several stems if you pinch out the top of the single stem when the plant is young. Or pinch out the terminal buds on every branch of a fuchsia. This forces the growth into other buds, and you soon have bushy growth from three or four new side branches where there was only one before.

Make each cut above a bud on a small side branch or main stem, or even to the ground level in the case of plants with several stems. Generally, it is preferable to prune so that you direct the growth of the new branch toward an open space rather than toward another branch; crossing branches tend to give a plant a cluttered, twiggy look.

When pruning, never leave a stub. Leaving excess wood to wither on stems is asking for invasion from pests or decay. Use pruners sharp enough to make a good clean cut.

• **Pruning for special effects.** For profuse blooms on your container plants, prune them in plenty of time for new flower buds to set. To encourage larger individual fruits, thin developing ones shortly after they form.

Character pruning isn't difficult, but more than a cursory glance is necessary to estimate a plant's potential. Study it from all angles, and probe under the foliage to discover hidden branch structure before you start cutting.

Going bare root—economical, easy

Bare root planting is a method—and usually the best method—of planting deciduous plants (those that lose their leaves in winter, such as roses, apples, or sycamores). Commercial growers raise the plants to salable size in their fields. Then in early December they dig up the plants, clean and trim the roots, and ship the plants off to nurseries.

Why buy bare root? Two reasons: 1) You save money. Typically a bare root plant costs only 30 to 70 percent of what it will cost later in the year. 2) A bare root plant is easier to maintain and often grows faster than it would if set out later in the year.

For bare root planting to be successful, the roots should be fresh (not half dead) and plump (not dry and withered), and in many cases the roots and tops should be pruned according to the kind of plant. Your experienced nurseryworker will be able to give you accurate and specific advice. If you have any doubts about the freshness of the roots, soak them overnight in a bucket of water before planting.

Roots *of newly purchased bare root rose bush are pruned so that they reach half the distance to bottom of container when bud union is at rim.*

Cover drainage hole *with shard, add soil. Lower rose into pot so bud union is level with rim. Fill in with new potting mix, leaving an inch at top for watering. Soak pot from below in tub of water.*

Weather protection

Because containers are exposed to the elements on all sides, potted plants are more sensitive to temperature changes than those in the ground. However, the portability of some containers can cancel out this disadvantage—they can be moved to escape weather extremes.

Here are a few hints for protecting plants during dry, hot, or windy weather: Keep plants well watered, moving them if possible to a sheltered spot under an overhang or shade tree. It's best to keep containers away from areas where they would receive reflected heat.

In cold-weather areas, check newspapers and radio or television reports daily for frost warnings. Move portable containers to protected spots not exposed to open sky. Small containers that can't be moved can be covered with cardboard boxes—just keep the lids closed at night and open during the day. For larger plants or those in containers too heavy to move, cover with plastic film, burlap, or even newspaper. Make sure the covering doesn't touch the foliage, though, because heat would be lost from the leaves through the point of contact. In the morning, or as soon as temperatures rise above freezing, remove covering.

What to do when your pot goes to pieces

A broken pot need not share the same fate as Humpty Dumpty. Using one of the superweatherproof glues, you can quickly and inexpensively repair most pots damaged by frost, wind, children, animals, or your own mishaps. When you're through, you may find that the strongest part of the glued-together pot is the crack.

You have your choice of two types of menders: epoxy glue or a fixture adhesive (neoprene mastic). Epoxy glue comes in a two-part package—either two tubes (about 1 ounce each) or two half-pint cans. One part is glue and the other a hardener. (For smaller jobs, the tubes are fine, but for larger jobs or for repairing a number of pots, choose the half-pint size.) After thoroughly mixing equal parts of glue and hardener, apply it to both surfaces of the pot pieces. Epoxy will dry clear.

The fixture adhesive requires no mixing at all and is almost as strong as epoxy. It dries to a tan color, closely matching the color of a terra cotta pot. Follow the directions on the label, being careful to work outdoors or in a very well-ventilated room. Wear disposable plastic gloves to keep glue off your hands. Don't mix more epoxy than you can use in about 45 minutes (you'll need less than you think and you'll find it takes some time to coat both surfaces of a large pot).

Rope, nylon cord, wire, or masking tape will hold the pot together as the glue hardens. Scrape away any excess glue that has oozed out of the cracks, especially around the outside where you'll see it. Sandpaper off any dried excess—this smooths edges and also colors the crack on unglazed pots.

It helps to have someone push the sections of big pots together while you bind them with nylon cord. Masking tape holds smaller pot at right.

If a cold spell catches your plants without protection and they freeze, take them to a garage or lighted cellar first thing in the morning, before the sun starts to thaw them. (The temperature of the shelter should be cold, but above freezing.) Allow the plants to thaw as slowly as possible.

Pliable *mesh wire or clear plastic is stretched around support stakes; cover plants with straw, if necessary.*

Newspaper *wrapped around staked wooden frame insulates smaller plants against cold evenings.*

Protect roses *where ground freezes by mounding soil over trunk. If it gets really cold, add conifer boughs or straw for more protection.*

Tack chicken wire *to a stake, using wire as tall as your plant and long enough to form cylinder around it. Put stake into ground next to plant, circle it with wire, and secure ends. Pack cylinder with straw.*

Common pests and diseases

Pests and diseases can attack container plants. We've listed below the most common of these, along with possible solutions.

A more obvious remedy, though, is often overlooked—preventing the problem in the first place. So here is a checklist of good gardening practices you can refer to from time to time:
• Examine all plants, new and established, before potting them. Look for signs of existing or potential pests or diseases.
• Use clean containers and sterilized potting mixes whenever you plant or transplant container subjects.
• Keep your containers free of weeds, fallen fruit, and dead flowers.
• Don't try to salvage severely diseased plants. They should be discarded (and not in a compost pile).
• Know your plants. Supply them with the growing conditions they need. Pests and diseases are less likely to attack healthy, well-established plants.

Pests

● **Ants.** Common crawling insects, usually red or black. Though ants don't harm plants directly, their nests often damage plant roots. Some ants attract other pests like aphids and mealybugs. *Remedy:* Kill ants by hand or use malathion spray.

● **Aphids.** Pests with soft, round bodies, usually green or reddish black. Clustering on buds or on new growth, they suck plant juices, causing stunted growth and a distorted leaf or flower appearance. *Remedy:* Hose aphids off or wash plant with a soapy (not detergent) solution. Pyrethrum or rotenone can also be used if needed.

● **Earwigs.** Crawling insects with long brownish bodies, and pincers protruding from their tails. They attack plants at night, chewing both leaves and flowers. *Remedy:* Remove earwigs from plants by hand or use malathion spray.

● **Leafhoppers.** Small, quick-moving brown or green insects. They suck plant juices from stems and leaves, causing a white stippling visible on the upper side of the leaf. *Remedy:* Hose leafhoppers off or spray them with pyrethrum or rotenone.

● **Mealybugs.** Round, white, fuzzy-bodied insects that live in colonies on leaf stems or in branch crotches. They suck plant juices, causing stunted growth (eventually may kill plant). *Remedy:* Touch mealybugs with a cotton swab dipped in alcohol, or hose them off with water. If necessary, spray them with petroleum oils.

● **Scale insects.** Round or oval bodies, usually brown or gray, have hard shell covering in adult stages. They form colonies that attack leaves and stems, causing stunted growth. Some scale insects secrete honeydew that gives leaves a shiny surface and promotes growth of sooty mold. *Remedy:* Scrape off insects with fingernails or a knife. Or wash them off with a soapy (not detergent) solution. In some cases, petroleum oils may be effective, but check labels first.

● **Snails, slugs.** Probably the most common, most destructive pests. At night and on overcast days, both can be found eating plant leaves. Look for a trail of silvery slime. *Remedy:* Pick off by hand or sprinkle ashes around the base of plants. If necessary, use bait—meal and pellet forms actually attract snails and slugs. Metaldehyde forms are best because when mixed with bran, they are not harmful to birds and pets.

● **Spider mites.** Flat, oval bodies, usually red or white; detectable only in groups or by the typical webbing effect they leave on foliage. Some leaves also become mottled with brown or yellow dots. *Remedy:* Isolate infested plants. Wash off the area with a soapy (not detergent) solution. If necessary, apply dusting sulfur or petroleum oils.

● **Thrips.** Small, fast-moving, with slender bodies in colors of tan, brown, and black with lighter colored markings. They often fly when disturbed and feed on foliage and flowers. *Remedy:* Hose thrips off. If necessary, apply pyrethrum, rotenone, or petroleum oils.

● **Whiteflies.** Common both indoors and out. Small white flying pest attaches and feeds on underside of leaves. Foliage turns yellow and is covered with a shiny, sticky layer of honeydew. *Remedy:* Hose off with water or apply a soapy (not detergent) solution. Many other insects feed on whiteflies, and they may solve the problem for you. If necessary, apply pyrethrum, rotenone, or petroleum oils.

Diseases

● **Crown or root rot.** Plants infected turn brown and mushy or suddenly collapse. Problem usually caused by overwatering or poor drainage. Repotting may be the only way to save your plant. *Remedy:* Correcting your watering habits is the best known control for this disease.

● **Damping off.** Newly sprouted seedlings develop a stem rot near the soil surface and fall off (some seeds fail to sprout at all). *Remedy:* Clean flats and containers thoroughly before using them. Plant with sterilized potting mixes.

● **Leaf spot, leaf blight, shot hole.** Red, brown, and yellow spots appear on leaves and stems. In some cases, the spots drop out, leaving a "shot hole" condition. *Remedy:* Isolate or discard diseased plant. Disease caused by airborne or waterborne fungi found generally in plant refuse, dead leaves, or fruit.

● **Powdery mildew.** Bluish white dust appears on leaves and flower buds. Foliage is curled and distorted. *Remedy:* Because the main cause is overwatering and poor air circulation, first move the plant to a better location; then change or correct your watering habits. After removing any damaged portion, spray the infected area with sulfur dust or benomyl.

● **Rust.** Blisters (from moisture) form on undersides of leaves, then scatter reddish or yellow spores about. *Remedy:* Remove infected areas and sporing bodies.

Moving the big ones

The first time you bend down to move a good-size container plant, you make two quick discoveries: the container is usually hard to get hold of, and the whole thing is much heavier than you expected.

You may start looking for some mechanical aids when you learn that a 12-inch clay pot of freshly watered petunias, for instance, can weigh 65 pounds. A rhododendron in an 18-inch square box weighs up to 200 pounds. The first rule is to move containers *before* watering to avoid the extra weight.

- **Lifting.** If you decide that you are able to lift a container, be sure you do it with your back straight. To avoid back strain, keep your back vertical and let your legs do the lifting. Attaching handles to the box also simplifies the job.

- **Skids and shovels.** Dragging a tub over a patio or down a walk is often the hardest way to move it. It isn't so much the weight as the friction that makes it difficult. Often all you need is to reduce the friction and get a good hold on the container.

A wide-blade shovel under a heavy tub will slide along well across the ground, lawn, or exposed aggregate. Don't use it, though, on a surface of brick or other material that might be scratched by the shovel. A wide-blade, D-handle coal shovel works well.

Professional movers skid heavy furniture across a surface on tough burlap strips. You can apply the same technique to heavy plant moving by placing a burlap bag or an old throw rug under it. Surprisingly, it pulls quite easily.

- **Rollers.** Using three or four rollers is the traditional Japanese method of moving a heavy container. Dowels or lengths of 2-inch pipe can be used. As the box is moved along over the dowels, take up a roller from behind and put it in front. You can turn corners easily by fanning out rollers at the turn. Rollers are not easy to use on a slope or on rough ground, though.

- **Wheels.** Three or four 2-inch industrial casters mounted on 1-inch plywood make satisfactory dollies for heavy loads. It may take two people to lift a box a few inches off the ground in order to slip the dolly underneath, but once that's done, the load is easy to move and is well balanced. Some casters can be attached permanently to the bottoms of containers.

A mover's two-wheeled hand truck, available from an equipment rental firm, will shift very heavy containers to new positions. In a container garden, especially where the effect is dependent on the frequent moving of plants, a hand truck proves to be a worthwhile investment.

Shovel blade *under a container load supplies a smooth sliding surface, reduces friction.*

Roll *containers about using a series of parallel pipes or sturdy dowels.*

Strong metal *hand trucks with good wheel bearings make dependable vehicles for container gardens.*

Flattened *cardboard carton (fold edge for handle) placed under container makes it easier to drag across lawn or soft ground.*

Living bouquets—eye-level and eye-catching

Container gardening gets an uplifting look with a flower display like this one. The aerial bouquet is actually flowering plants grown in a moss-lined wire basket. The plants grow from the sides and bottom as well as in the top, creating a whole sphere (or half sphere) of color.

To make a living bouquet, you need a few bedding plants, a package of green moss or sphagnum moss, and a wire basket. (Do not use a basket smaller than 14 inches—it dries out too fast.)

Place the plants closer together than you would if planting in the ground—about 3 to 6 inches apart. If you start with plants that already have blooms on them (as in the photographs), the basket should look pretty good in about 2 or 3 weeks.

Water every other day, or daily if the weather is hot or windy. You can make sure the basket is completely damp by filling the top several times until excess drips from the bottom.

Frequent feeding is absolutely essential to keep the bouquets alive and blooming. A complete fertilizer (high in nitrogen) should be applied 2 weeks after planting and then every 2 weeks without fail.

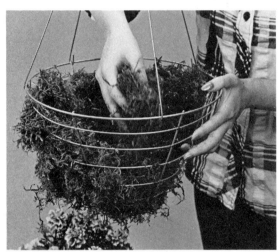

Soak moss *and push through mesh from inside. Make moss lining 1 inch thick and 1 inch higher than basket rim.*

Make planting holes *in moss with fingers or shears. Push roots through from outside while pulling them from inside.*

After filling lowest tier, *add enough lightweight potting soil to cover roots of plants completely in that tier.*

Finally, *plant the top. Basket here has dwarf French marigolds, petunias, and sweet alyssum on sides, big marigolds on top.*

Simple containers to make

Disguise a 5-gallon nursery can by slipping it into a rough-sawn redwood jacket. Box planters are assembled with lag screws in predrilled holes. Collar pieces rest on can.

Two containers from one barrel—deep end, 23½ inches high, holds large tree; shallow end, just 9 inches deep, holds enough soil to support flowering annuals.

Nursery flats of flowering annuals create instant color for most garden areas. Overlapping bricks (left), stacked two high, surround flat. Shelf of bottomless wood frame (above) supports nursery flat.

More containers to make

If you have decided to build a container yourself, more than likely the material you've chosen is wood. It's durable and easy to work with, and it adapts easily to almost any design.

Redwood and cedar are the most widely used woods in container construction because they resist decay and weather attractively with little or no outside finish. Douglas fir is stronger than these and is therefore suitable for very large planters. But it should be stained on the outside to discourage discoloration and treated on the inside with a wood preservative if you wish it to last more than a few years.

If you accept the challenge to build your container—and perhaps even design it, too—it's well worth a little extra time to guarantee pleasing results. We've listed a few helpful tips that apply to containers constructed of wood:

Use lumber at least 1 inch thick.

Assemble boards so the grain runs in one direction. If boards warp, they won't leave large gaps.

Glue (make sure it's waterproof) and nail the corners. Use screws for extra strength.

Paint the inside and the bottom with a wood preservative, or waterproof with an inside coating of asphalt emulsion or tree sealer. Or line the container with plastic sheeting, stapled to fit snugly.

Be sure to apply a protective finish unless container is made from redwood or cedar—those woods can be left in their natural condition.

2 x 12

20″

12″

2 x 4s

A simple square box *takes on added interest when overlapped edges are notched to fit exactly. Notches are cut 2 inches from top and bottom and 4 inches deep. Sides of container rest on a bottom of 2 by 4s, cut slightly shorter on all sides. Five 3/4-inch holes are drilled in bottom for drainage.*

Build this container *by stacking 2 by 10s for sides, adding 2 by 2s on inside corners. Sides rest on a 2-inch bottom, cut slightly shorter on all sides. Grooved design is made with router or table saw with dado blade. Five 3/4-inch holes drilled in bottom provide drainage.*

2 x 2s

2 x 10s

20″

20″

1/2″ x 1/2″ grooves

2″ bottom

Trim attached with nails driven from inside

18″

2″ x 4″ cap

12″

2″ bottom

2 x 12s

1″ lath trim

2″ lath trim (vertical)

2″ lath trim (horizontal)

Start with a simple box, *then add outside trim (using 1 or 2-inch lath) and 2 by 4 cap. Assemble base, then nail on 2 by 12 sides. Drive nails for vertical trim from inside to avoid showing. Use both glue and nails to hold mitered joints of cap together. Drill five 3/4-inch drainage holes in bottom.*

5/16″ x 1-1/2″ x 1-1/2″ lath spacers

20-1/2″

25″

Redwood 2 x 2s

3/4″ plywood box

4 x 4s

Staggered lag bolts

25-1/2″

20″

10-1/2″-long lath, glued on edge

3/4″ plywood box

Both containers *(above, right) begin with a 17½ by 17½ by 20-inch box of 3/4-inch exterior plywood. This one features 25-inch-long redwood 2 by 2s separated by 5/16-inch lath spacers. Finishing nails secure 2 by 2s to plywood. Design: James Kramer.*

Same basic box—just different trim. Here, fir 4 by 4s are held together by sturdy lag bolts. Sides of plywood box are faced with lath strips set on edge and glued together. Design: James Kramer.*

1 x 12 rough-sawn redwood (or cedar)

2″ bottom

12″

36″

14″

Two sides *of this container butt over the other two—usual box construction. Sides rest on a 2-inch bottom, cut slightly short on all sides. Use long, thin galvanized or cement-coated nails for maximum holding power without splitting. For drainage, drill 3/4-inch holes in bottom.*

Homemade containers   37

Plants That Like Container Life

Garden room *explodes with color of begonias, geraniums, impatiens, petunias, lobelia.*

Almost any plant you take a fancy to will adapt to container living, at least for a time. During your next nursery visit, take a little extra time to look for plants with *special* appeal—a unique branching habit, interesting foliage, or lovely flower color. Even a tender or temperamental plant is likely to grow in a container, because you can place it in a favored location and give it the particular care it requires.

The plants described on the following pages are especially suited to container life. Some are familiar favorites; others may be new to you. Our lists include annuals, perennials, bulbs, vines, shrubs and trees, hanging and indoor plants, fruits, vegetables, herbs, and such specialties as ferns, bonsai, and pool plants.

Remember that these lists are not intended to be all-inclusive. If some other plant intrigues you as a tub subject, give it a try. Opportunities for experimentation and personal satisfaction are almost unlimited.

Annuals—color for a season

For a quick, refreshing change, an added splash of color, or a filler while permanent plants mature, why not liven up your garden with annuals? Most adapt well to the confines of containers—pots, boxes, tubs, or hanging baskets. Their single-season life span makes them temporary plants that look most attractive when flowers are in bloom. And bloom they will, week after week, without the year-round attention long-lived varieties require.

Using basic potting mix (page 24), transplant annuals from flats available at your nursery. Or, to grow your own plants from seed, sow seeds directly into permanent containers filled with moist soil, then cover them with a thin layer of equal parts of sand and potting mix. Keep pots shaded until seeds have germinated. Water regularly and give a light monthly feeding of complete fertilizer.

Not all the plants included in our list are true annuals. Some are biennials that flower during the first year; others (indicated by *) are tender perennials that live from year to year only in ideal climates. Elsewhere, these types are treated as annuals, so we've listed them here. For quick reference, we begin each listing with the height of the plant, its blooming season, and the best location for good growth.

African Daisy
6–12" • Winter, spring bloom • Sun

Glossy, daisylike flowers bloom in abundance on low, spreading mounds. Flowers open only in full sun, close at night and on cloudy days. Unsurpassed for color in dry-winter areas.

Ageratum (Floss Flower)
6–12" • Summer bloom • Sun

Choose pink or lavender blue floss flowers to highlight a tub of cascading white petunias or sweet alyssum.

Where summers are long, locate on east side of house or in a lightly shaded area.

Alyssum, Sweet
6–8" • Spring, summer bloom • Sun

Clusters of tiny white or rose-colored flowers spread in a low-branching, trailing way. Fast growing, with a fragrance like honey, alyssum contrasts well with colorful annuals in pots or hanging baskets.

Amethyst Flower, see Browallia

Aster, China
8–36" • Summer bloom • Sun

Plant dwarf or cushion varieties by themselves or in mixed bouquets. Sturdy upright stems support long-lasting flowers in shades of red, purple, and white. To prevent diseases such as aster wilt or yellows, avoid overwatering.

*Baby's Breath
8–24" • Summer bloom • Sun

Sprays of delicate single-flower blooms add an airy charm to larger, textured plants in mixed bouquets. Try in combination with golden marigolds or bright red zinnias. Plants grow fast but last only 6 weeks; sow seeds often for continuous bloom.

Bachelor's Button (Cornflower)
8–24" • Spring bloom • Sun

Known for its soft, silver gray foliage, this branched, bushy plant produces an abundance of rayed pastel blossoms throughout spring. Compact dwarf varieties such as 'Polka Dot' do well in tubs or large pots.

Balsam, see Impatiens

Browallia (Amethyst Flower)
8–24" • Summer, autumn bloom • Shade

Clusters of lobelialike flowers appear throughout summer and autumn. Choose a warm, shady spot for such free-blooming varieties as *B. americana* 'Sapphire'. Blue or violet flowers look attractive grouped with begonias or soft-colored fuchsias.

Calendula
6–12" • Spring, autumn bloom • Sun

Cheery blooms in yellow, orange, apricot, and tangerine bring a splash of color to winter gardens in mild areas. For successive flowering, pinch back main stem occasionally. Watch out for snails and slugs—they adore calendulas.

Canary-Bird Flower, see Nasturtium

Pastel snapdragons *complement flared red clay container.*

Adobe corner *boasts 'Dancy' tangerine with purple lobelia carpet, pots of marigolds.*

Bright *red, pink, and white phlox spill over sides of low terra cotta pot.*

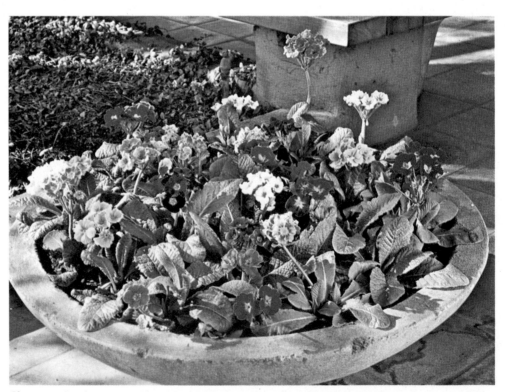

Clusters *of color are Pacific primroses (Primula polyantha). Mass them in low container.*

*Candytuft

6-15" • Spring bloom • Sun

Fragrant mounds of white and pastel flowers grow easily from seed in spring or late autumn. Display them in pots grouped near spring bulbs such as daffodils or tulips. To stimulate new growth, shear top of plant lightly after first bloom.

Celosia (Cockscomb)

6-36" • Summer bloom • Sun

A container of scarlet cockscomb plumes mixed with masses of white petunias can be spectacular. Give them full sun; water and fertilize regularly. An excellent choice for dry desert areas.

*Cineraria

12-15" • Spring bloom • Shade

Daisylike flowers—usually in bright colors with contrasting eyes—bloom in cool, shaded spots. Seeds may be sown in place or seedlings transplanted from flats. On warm days, mist foliage to help prevent wilting.

Cockscomb, see Celosia

*Coleus

1-3' • Summer, autumn bloom • Sun

Spectacular foliage—usually several colors to a leaf—characterizes this indoor/outdoor plant. High-nitrogen fertilizer, plenty of water, and strong indirect light produce the vivid colors. Cuttings root easily in water.

Multicolored *foliage of coleus becomes more vivid in strong indirect light.*

Cornflower, see Bachelor's Button

Cosmos

2-6' • Summer bloom • Sun

Tall, thin stems with feathery foliage support daisylike bicolored blooms—usually red, white, pink, or lavender flowers with tufted yellow centers. A good background plant in mixed bouquets with other showy annuals.

*Fairy Primrose

12-15" • Winter, spring bloom • Shade

Lacy, long-stemmed blooms in gentle pastels add cheerful color to midwinter gardens. Mass them in pots under a shading tree or display them near early-flowering spring bulbs. These hardy plants withstand light frost but must be kept moist and protected from drying winds.

Floss Flower, see Ageratum

Impatiens (Balsam)

8-24" • Summer bloom • Filtered sun

Showy, often bicolored, single or double flowers bloom in profusion on bushy plants. Nicknamed "touch-me-not," impatiens thrives in warm, sunny spots during summer and early autumn. Before first frost, try bringing a few plants indoors for winter bloom.

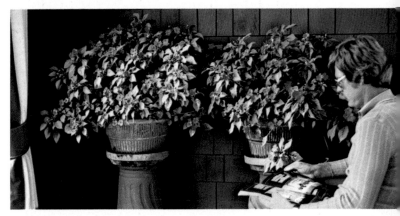

Twin *terra cotta pots hold orange single impatiens. Design: W. David Poot.*

Lobelia

4-8" • Spring, autumn bloom • Sun

Dainty blue flowers growing in low, spreading mounds make lobelia an outstanding choice for containers. Use as a cascade edging in mixed bouquets or plant with bright-colored annuals in hanging baskets.

*Madagascar Periwinkle (Vinca Rosea)

1-2' • Summer bloom • Sun

Hardy, dependable, and heat-loving—that's the Madagascar periwinkle. Ideal for desert or long-summer areas. Its phloxlike flowers, in plain white or with contrasting red centers, may bloom continuously from early summer until frost.

Marigold

6-36" • Summer, autumn bloom • Sun

Display tall, sturdy-stemmed varieties in large containers; mass compact French marigolds in small pots or use them in mixed bouquets. Long-lasting blooms first appear in summer in all shades of yellow, orange, red, and white. Plants enjoy frequent watering, but not from above.

*Nasturtium (Canary-Bird Flower)

8-48" • Summer, autumn bloom • Sun

These are easy to grow when seeds or young plants are placed directly in containers. Bushy dwarf varieties reach 15 inches high; trailing types climb a trellis 4 feet or more. Brilliantly colored flowers appear throughout summer.

Nemesia

10-18" • Spring, summer bloom • Sun

Try combining vivid, warm colors of nemesia with cascading lobelia, sweet alyssum, or violas. Bushy, rapid-growing plants reach 18 inches high and produce delicate flowers in spring and early summer. Keep soil moist but not soggy.

*Nicotiana

1-3' • Summer bloom • Sun

Clusters of fragrant, tubular flowers grow on 1 to 3-foot stems. For best effect, group four or more plants in each container. Tolerates considerable heat if given shade in the afternoon. 'Sensation Mixed' variety blooms in such unusual colors as lime, mauve, brown, and chartreuse.

*Pansy (Viola)

6-8" • Winter, spring bloom • Sun

Outstanding, ever-popular annuals offer long-lasting winter and spring color in mild regions, spring and summer color in cooler areas. Compact plants, usually less than 8 inches high, look handsome in hanging baskets and mixed bouquets or massed in low containers. For continuous, profuse bloom, pinch off old flowers, water and fertilize often.

*Petunia

6-12" • Summer bloom • Sun

Truly the ideal container plant. Showy, long-lasting, trumpet-shaped flowers in all colors but green thrive in most temperature zones. Trailing Cascade series makes an excellent choice for hanging baskets or for accompanying upright annuals in mixed bouquets.

Phlox

6-8" • Spring, summer, autumn bloom • Sun

In light, rich soil with full sun and ample watering, phlox blooms from early summer until frost. Plant it alone or use it to accent marigolds or zinnias in complementary shades. Some varieties produce frilled or starred flowers with contrasting centers.

*Primrose

6-12" • Winter, spring bloom • Shade

Primula polyantha, a perennial usually treated as an annual in containers, does best in rich, moist soil in a partially shaded location. Brilliant or pastel-colored flowers blooming on sturdy stems often last a month or more.

Scarlet Sage (Salvia)

1-3' • Summer, autumn bloom • Sun

Dazzling red color combines effectively with white-flowered or gray-foliaged plants. Good choices include daisies and petunias, since they also need a sunny location and regular waterings. Grows slowly from seed.

*Snapdragon

6-36" • Spring, summer bloom • Sun

In containers of mixed annuals, snapdragons are invaluable for vertical color. An attractive display combines pink snaps and petunias with rose-colored sweet alyssum. Rust can be a problem, so avoid overhead watering.

*Sweet Pea

6-12" • Winter, spring bloom • Sun

Fragrant, long-stemmed flowers in all colors but yellow grow on bushy or climbing vines. Compact types such as Bijou and Knee-Hi are best suited for low containers. Because plants are sensitive to heat, they should be soaked thoroughly when watered.

*Sweet William

10-30" • Spring, summer bloom • Sun

Gray green foliage and petals with notched edges distinguish this member of the carnation family. Plants are vigorous growers, tolerating frost but not extreme heat. Valuable in mixed bouquets, sweet William blooms in white and shades of red, pink, and purple.

Torenia (Wishbone Flower)

6-12" • Summer bloom • Sun

Add a subtle touch to shaded areas by displaying bicolored torenia in containers with fibrous begonias or trailing lobelia. Similar to gloxinia, this plant enjoys warm soil and high humidity.

*Verbena

6-12" • Summer bloom • Sun

Sun-loving and heat-resistant, verbena produces flat clusters of flowers growing from low, spreading stems. Available in a spectrum of colors, it is useful as a quick, effective "ground cover" in containers.

Vinca Rosea, see Madagascar Periwinkle

Viola, see Pansy

Wishbone Flower, see Torenia

Zinnia

6–36" • Summer bloom • Sun

Planted alone or in mixed containers, these hot-weather favorites bloom in most colors and sizes, including such small-flowering types as Thumbelina and Tom Thumb. They're subject to mildew, so try watering from above.

Hot-weather favorites, Zinnia elegans, *bloom in rainbow of colors, most with yellow centers.*

Perennials are dependable year after year

Even in the coldest climates, perennials are a hardy group. They offer seasonal color from year to year, usually in spring or summer. During the winter months, roots remain alive, but plants traditionally die back down to the soil's surface. However, in milder climates or when protected from threatening frosts, many perennials keep their foliage all year. Whichever is the case, there is a special advantage to growing perennials in pots—you can bring them on stage when they are at their best and put them behind the scenes once bloom has ended.

If grown or sold in pots, perennials can be transplanted at any time during the year, but you should wait until spring or autumn to transplant ones that have been dug up from the ground. Plant in a rich soil and place in a sunny location unless otherwise noted in our list. Start feeding with a complete fertilizer when new growth first appears, and apply monthly until flowers start to bloom.

Agapanthus

1–5' • Summer bloom • Sun

Blue, purple, or white flowers, clustered on tall stems, make a handsome display in large wooden or clay containers. Wide, strap-shaped foliage is attractive all year if kept well watered and protected from hottest sun. Choose dwarf varieties such as 'Peter Pan' for smaller containers.

Aster

1–3' • Spring, summer, autumn bloom • Sun

Red, blue, and purple flowers, usually with contrasting yellow eyes, are appealing planted alone or in mixed bouquets. Fragrant varieties such as 'Wonder of Stafa' or 'Jungfrau' are excellent choices for redwood tubs or wide clay pots. They propagate easily by dividing clumps in late fall or early spring.

Long-stemmed asters *in red, purple combination stand tall in half barrel.*

Begonia, Bedding or Wax

4–18" • Summer, autumn bloom • Filtered sun

Doubly attractive—the leaves are as colorful as the flowers. Single or double blooms appear in white, red, rose, or pink. Like most begonias, these enjoy somewhat humid surroundings but should be allowed to dry out between waterings. Protect from drying winds. (For hanging begonias, see page 71.)

Bird of Paradise

2–5' • Year-round bloom • Sun

Peering above clumps of flat, long-stalked leaves are spectacular orange, blue, and white flowers, said to resemble tropical birds. Plants thrive in most containers, blooming intermittently throughout the year when given frequent heavy doses of complete fertilizer.

Carnation, Border

12-18" • Spring, summer bloom • Sun

Halved oak barrels filled to capacity with colorful border carnations add a lively look to redwood decks or brick patios. These bushy, free-blooming plants are sun lovers, preferring rich, well-drained soil and occasional feedings. Take care not to overwater.

Chrysanthemum, Florists'

1-3' • Summer, autumn bloom • Sun

Popular, versatile choice for most containers. A variety of flower forms and colors are available, including cushion types that bloom heavily on compact, 12-inch mounds. For bushiness and continuous flowering, pinch back main stems occasionally.

Dusty Miller

1-2' • Summer bloom • Sun

Illuminate your patio on a dark day or a moonlit night with a container of dusty miller. Velvety white leaves grow in a compact, shrublike manner; clusters of purple or soft yellow blooms appear in midsummer. Trim back after flowering has finished.

Geranium

1-3' • Spring, summer, autumn bloom • Sun

One of the most common and easily adaptable perennials for container living. Some are scented; others have fancy leaves; many have bright blooms. Glossy ivy geraniums trail in hanging baskets; scented and Martha Washington varieties bloom best when slightly potbound.

Tepee—*fashioned from three bamboo poles lashed together—supports geraniums planted in wide-mouthed clay container.*

Hosta, see Plantain Lily

Marguerite

1-4' • Summer, autumn bloom • Sun

Long-lasting white and yellow daisies (blue on *Felicia*) appear throughout warm seasons on rounded, shrubby plants. Valuable for their rapid growth and prolific bloom, marguerites give quick, effective color in containers. Try massing them in redwood tubs or large clay pots.

Plantain Lily (Hosta)

1-2' • Summer bloom • Filtered sun

Accent a poolside or mixed-shade area with distinctive plantain lilies; for best effect, group three or more pots together. Although known for their glossy, heart-shaped foliage, they also produce white or mauve tubular flowers briefly during summer.

Shrubs and trees with flowers and foliage

Tubbed shrubs and small trees are as versatile as they are varied. Offering a natural, established look wherever placed, they enhance any garden setting, small or large. Conifers and other evergreens look attractive all year around and make good background plants for blooming annuals and perennials. Flowering shrubs and trees and those with blazing fall color or attractive berries stage a seasonal show all by themselves. Still others, because of their unique appeal, merit special display to dramatize their bold, colorful, or unusual foliage.

Almost any slow-growing shrub or small tree will tolerate container life for a while. With the few exceptions noted, they do best in a basic potting soil kept slightly on the dry side.

Flowering

Azalea

1-12' • Late winter, spring bloom • Filtered sun

One of the most spectacular container subjects available—superb beauty in flower, handsome foliage out of bloom. Gardeners in nearly every climate (except the desert) where winter temperatures do not fall below -15° can grow some kind of azalea in a container. Especially well adapted are Belgian Indica, Southern Indica, and Kurume kinds, but there are about a dozen different groups of azaleas, evergreen and deciduous, in red, pink, salmon, violet, and white. The best way to select one is to visit a nursery during the spring blooming season and find a shape, size, and bloom you want.

Generally, azaleas do best in acid mix (page 24) in a partly shaded spot protected from wind. Keep constantly moist but not soggy. Feed with acid plant food (some are labeled "azalea food") every 6 to 8 weeks, three or four times from the *end* of the flowering season until September. Prune at blooming time; pinch back new tips during the growing period to keep plants compact.

Bougainvillea

1-6' • Summer, autumn bloom • Sun

Low-growing, shrubby forms of this flowering, evergreen vine—'La Jolla', 'Temple Fire', and 'Crimson Jewel'—are best suited for container use. In summer, use them in a sunny patio; move to a protected spot in colder months when temperatures drop near freezing. Tender roots are easily damaged, so plant carefully. Water normally during growing season and fertilize in spring and summer.

Camellia

2-15' • Winter, spring bloom • Filtered sun

Spectacular flowers during cooler months combined with handsome foliage the year around make camellias container favorites. Colors are limited to red, pinks, white, and variegations, but the sizes and varieties are almost endless. *C. japonica* is *the* camellia to most gardeners, but delicately beautiful *C. sasanqua*, spectacular *C. reticulata*, and other kinds are worthy container subjects.

Using an acid soil mix (page 24), plant camellia, keeping trunk base just above soil line. Feed with commercial acid fertilizer after the blooming period, following label directions carefully. During growth season, water thoroughly; a thick mulch helps to keep plants constantly moist.

Cotoneaster

1-6' • Spring bloom • Sun

Stiffly angled, spreading branches of rock cotoneaster (*C. horizontalis*) make it a good candidate for a tubbed espalier or traffic barrier. *C. congesta* grows slowly, hugs the ground, does well in both hot and cold climates. Both types have small leaves, whitish flowers, and red berries; they thrive with little care.

Crape Myrtle

3-20' • Summer bloom • Sun

Soft clusters of pastel blooms and colorful fall foliage characterize this deciduous shrub. Flourishes in hot interiors and desert areas; tends to mildew where summers are cool. Dwarf forms such as 'Petite Embers' and 'Snow White' (5 to 7 feet) are best for containers. Water infrequently, thoroughly; feed every 2 months.

Daphne, Winter

1-5' • Winter bloom • Filtered sun

Liven up a midwinter garden with colorful daphne. Blooms are pink to deep red, with creamy pink throats. Neat and handsome, this evergreen shrub is valued for

its delightful fragrance. Somewhat temperamental—demands a fast-draining soil and protection from cold winds.

Flowering Fruit Trees

2-10' • Spring or summer bloom • Sun

With the exception of almond and peach, most deciduous flowering fruit trees make excellent container subjects—they have not only spectacular flowers but redeeming looks when not in bloom as well.

They thrive in fast-draining basic soil with ample moisture and regular feeding. Prune to shape at bloom time. Remember that these plants are *trees*; they should be placed in containers that balance their height. Once a tree reaches 8 to 10 feet, it may require transplanting to open ground.

Japanese flowering cherry. Spectacular spring blossoms in pink and white; beautiful branch structure when dormant. Attractive in almost any setting—entryways, patios, decks.

Flowering crabapple. The least troublesome of the flowering fruit trees, crabapples combine nicely with bulbs, primroses, or other shade-loving plants. Select smaller, slow-growing types—3 years in a 2-foot container is the average stay of a 6-foot tree.

Flowering plum. Spring-blooming flowers are fragrant, bright pink; leaves are reddish purple, turning to bronze in summer. A 3-foot tree can remain in a 12-inch box for 2 years.

Flowering quince. Beautiful, hardy, and easy to grow. White, pink, or red flowers appear in earliest spring on unusually structured angular branches. Effective when displayed by itself in a prominent spot.

The dwarf forms of trees producing edible fruits are also excellent container subjects. See page 59.

Fuchsia

1-5' • Summer, autumn bloom • Filtered sun or shade

Showy flowers—pink, red, white, violet, and variegations—dangle from stems. Flowers come in a variety of sizes, and though they lack fragrance, passing hummingbirds always stop for a visit. Select upright kinds for boxes and tubs, trailing kinds for hanging baskets and espaliers.

Planted in rich, fast-draining soil, fuchsias thrive in cool garden spots or under shady patio overhangs. They prefer mild summer climates, but you can create a pleasant humid atmosphere for them with wind and sun protection and attentive watering—often twice a day in warm areas. In cold-winter areas, containers should be moved to a protected area and mulched heavily.

If you live in a frostless area, prune back in spring to within two buds of previous summer's growth. In colder areas, wait until after last frost; then cut back to live wood by carefully removing twiggy growth. In severe-winter areas, fuchsias are often treated as annuals.

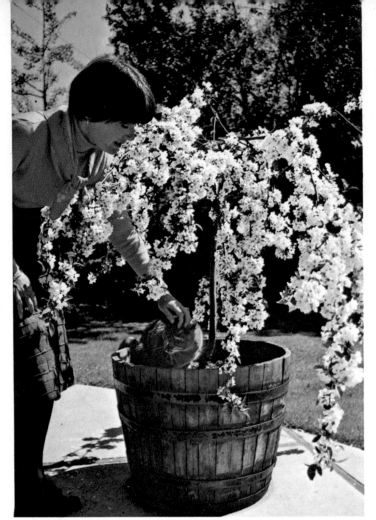

White-blossomed *flowering crabapple is graceful touch.*

Bright *pink azalea, trained into standard, gets annual pruning, monthly feeding.*

Gardenia

1-5' • Summer, autumn bloom • Sun or filtered sun

Bright green, glossy foliage and deeply-scented, waxy white flowers characterize gardenias. The best known variety, *G. jasminoides* 'Mystery', has double white flowers and reaches 4 to 5 feet; *G.j.* 'Veitchii', with prolific inch-wide blooms, is a compact 3-foot plant. All take full sun in coastal areas, filtered sun inland; water them frequently and heavily and feed often.

Holly

2-10' • Autumn berries • Sun or filtered sun

A pot of growing holly, with or without traditional berries, is an attractive indoor/outdoor plant—especially at holiday time. Usually, both male and female plants must be planted for the female to bear fruit. Holly prefers a rich, slightly acidic soil, sun, and ample watering. English holly *(Ilex aquifolium)* is the traditional Christmas holly; Chinese holly *(I. cornuta* 'Burfordii Nana') is self-pollinating and has exceptionally large berries.

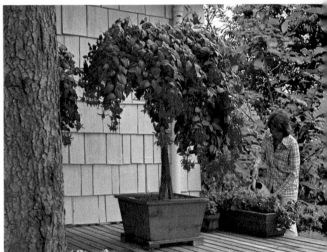

Cascading *fuchsia, 17 years old, receives filtered shade, semimonthly feeding.*

Potted *bougainvillea flank steps of desert home.*

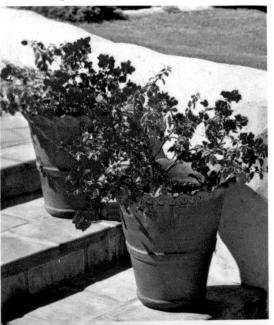

Hydrangea

2-8' • Summer, autumn bloom • Sun or filtered sun

For a lively display through summer months, mass containers of hydrangeas on decks or near entries. Color ranges from white through blues to purple and red. They're easy to grow in rich, porous soil but require heavy, regular watering. Fertilize three or four times during the growing season. Size can be controlled by pruning at bloom time.

To get blue flowers on pink and red varieties, or to keep blue-flowered kinds from turning, treat with a solution of aluminum sulfate (1 tablespoon in a gallon of water); make two or three applications before the plant blooms.

Mahonia Lomariifolia

2-8' • Winter bloom • Filtered sun

These showy plants have interesting, vertical branch structure and spiny, glossy leaves. Clusters of yellow flowers appear in winter, followed by powdery blue berries. Afternoon shade helps to keep foliage deep green.

Oleander

2-12' • Summer, autumn bloom • Sun

Large clusters of white, pink, yellow, or red blooms appear on woody, leafy stems. Because it grows quickly and tolerates heat, oleander is one of the best evergreen shrubs for hot inland or desert areas. With sufficient pruning, it can be held to moderate size in a tub for years. Needs protection from severe cold winters. *Caution:* all parts are poisonous if eaten.

Pyracantha

1-10' • Summer bloom, autumn berries • Sun

Popular, dependable pyracanthas are grown for their bright scarlet berries and rugged, informal effect. *P.* 'Rosedale', with its tiny cream-colored flowers and bright red berries, can be trained as a standard or espaliered. Compact, 3-foot 'Tiny Tim' is thornless, well suited for a tubbed barrier. Both need full sun and a basic soil mix kept on the dry side.

Rhododendron

1-8' • Spring bloom • Filtered sun or shade

Well-tended, blooming rhododendrons can be a flower extravaganza in deep red, bluish pink, creamy white, yellow, and near-blue—and all variations in between. Because of similar growing requirements, they combine well with azaleas, many ferns, and other shade-loving plants. Locate tubbed rhododendrons under trees, near protected entryways, on north or east sides of buildings and fences, or under lath overhangs.

Plant in a rich, acidic soil mix (page 24), keeping it constantly moist yet well drained. (*If* drainage is good, it is almost impossible to overwater a rhododendron.) After blooming has finished, feed monthly until August with acid fertilizer (often called "azalea food" or "rhododendron food").

For planting in containers—wooden tubs, half barrels, clay pots—select compact 3 to 4-foot varieties such as white-flowered 'Bric-a-Brac', bright red 'Britannia', and lavender blue 'Blue Diamond'.

Rose

1-4' • Summer, autumn bloom • Sun

No other flowering shrub is so widely planted or beloved as the rose. Its hardiness, versatility, and growing habits make it a favorite among container gardeners.

Buy only healthy, top quality roses suited to your climate. Using a basic soil mix, plant them in boxes, half barrels, tubs, or clay pots; but remember that their roots should not be cramped. Use containers large enough to accommodate the roots when they are spread out.

Locate in full or half-day sun where air circulation is good. Soak thoroughly every few days, perhaps daily during hot spells. Feed roses with a complete fertilizer just as growth begins in spring, again after the main blooming period, and once more when the plant begins to put out growth for a fall crop of flowers. For pest and disease control and pruning ideas, see the *Sunset* book *How to Grow Roses.*

Roses have vigorous root systems. Every 3 or 4 years, remove plants from containers during the winter dormant period and trim 2 to 3 inches from the matted sides and bottom of the root ball. Replace in the same tub or, if you wish, a larger one, adding fresh new soil at the bottom and sides of tub. Soak thoroughly and apply a mulch to retain moisture.

Polyanthas and Floribundas—low-growing roses that produce flowers in large clusters—are especially popular for containers. 'The Fairy', pink, and 'Margo Koster', coral orange, are two good Polyanthas with a cascading or trailing habit. 'Sarabande', red, 'Roman Holiday', orange-red, and 'Border Gem', yellow, are good Floribundas.

If you enjoy miniature roses, try 'Eleanor', with tiny pink double flowers; it is particularly popular as an indoor/outdoor container plant.

Hybrid Teas also do well in containers, but for a pleasing effect, avoid the tall, lanky varieties.

Shrimp Plant

1-4' • Spring bloom • Filtered sun

The unusual appearance of tubular "shrimps" (actually white flowers enclosed in overlapping copper-colored bracts) makes this an interesting plant for entry or patio. It grows to a 3 to 4-foot mound but can be kept lower and more compact by diligent pinching in early growth. It needs winter protection in colder areas.

Yesterday-Today-and-Tomorrow

1-5' • Early summer bloom • Filtered sun

Flowers quickly change colors—purple one day, violet the next, and nearly white the next—hence the name.

White flower spikes *of twin yuccas contrast with dark balcony, walls. Design: W. David Poot.*

Changing *seasons tint leaves, branches of Japanese maple (Acer palmatum).*

Bowl-like *aggregate container holds Japanese maple; ground cover, orange impatiens at base. Design: W. David Poot.*

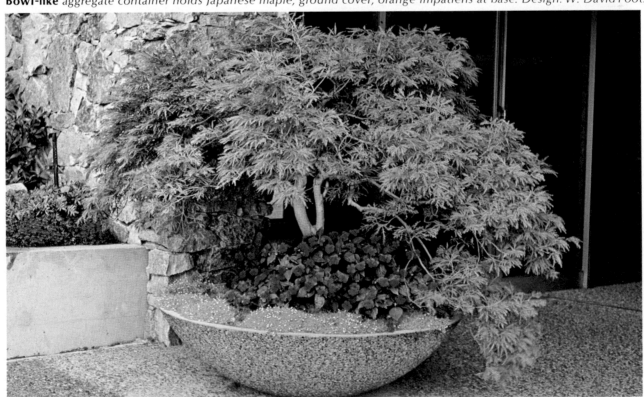

This handsome evergreen does best in rich, slightly acidic soil mix. It enjoys regular watering and feeding with complete fertilizer. With frequent pruning, size can be held to 3 feet.

Yucca

4-10' • Summer bloom • Sun

A dramatic choice for a desert garden with cacti and succulents, *Yucca recurvifolia* has blue gray leaves 3 feet long and a white flower spike. Easy to grow in a sandy mix; will withstand considerable drought and drying winds.

Foliage

Aralia, Japanese

3-10' • Filtered sun or shade

A look of the tropics—glossy, fanlike leaves up to 15 inches wide on long, swaying stems. Popular as an indoor plant where temperatures are low or outdoors where winters remain mild. Place container in a shady area; water and feed regularly during growing season.

Bamboo

4-30' • Sun or filtered sun

Ideal for Oriental effects in the garden, tubbed bamboo also makes an attractive sun screen or a living wall on patios and decks. It can be pruned or thinned to any desired size; it thrives in most conditions except hottest afternoon sun. Keeping bamboo lush and green is easy—water and feed it regularly, replant every 2 or 3 years before spreading roots become hard.

Black bamboo. Grows 4 to 8 feet; stems vary from pure black to olive-dotted black.

Chinese goddess bamboo. Dwarf variety, growing 4 to 6 feet with tiny leaves in fernlike sprays.

Golden bamboo. Thick foliage on 6 to 10-foot stems is ideal for screens. Frequent watering keeps it attractive.

Heavenly bamboo, Sacred bamboo. Characterized by crimson winter leaves, sturdy canes, lacy foliage; slow-growing to 6 to 8 feet. A good selection for restricted vertical area or wherever delicate, upright display is needed.

Palmate bamboo. Spreading, fingerlike foliage up to 15 inches long by 4 inches wide; mature plant reaches 4 to 5 feet.

Phyllostachys viridis. Tall, curving stems with ferny growth at base. Grows to 15 to 20 feet; good choice for a narrow space or as a barrier.

Bay, Sweet

3-20' • Sun or filtered sun

Also known as Grecian laurel, this classical, formal tree bears the traditional bay leaf for cookery. Often pruned into topiary shapes—spheres, cones, and so

forth—bays are valued as being hardy, dependable, and evergreen.

Beech

5-35' • Sun or filtered sun

Smooth gray bark and glossy green leaves which turn brown in autumn make the deciduous beech a handsome container subject. Select from tricolor beech (with green leaves edged in white and pink), golden beech, or weeping copper beech, which has purple leaves. All thrive in good, well-drained soil and produce feeder roots near the surface; avoid disturbing with deep cultivation.

Boxwood

2-15' • Sun or shade

Vivid green foliage of *Buxus* in containers is often trimmed to formal shapes; when not clipped, it grows soft and billowing. Plant slow-growing Japanese boxwood in hot, dry areas; in colder locations, try Korean boxwood or the lustrous English (common) boxwood.

Cedar, Deodar

3-10' • Sun

This popular conifer grows in low, spreading form. Only compact varieties—*Cedrus deodara* 'Prostrata', which is flat or cascading, and *C. d.* 'Repandens', with stiff horizontal branches— are small enough for lengthy container life. Prune to shape each year in late spring.

Fir

5-40' • Sun or filtered sun

Two handsome varieties—Nordmann fir, densely covered with dark green needles, and white fir, with 2-inch bluish green needles—adapt better to container life and warmer climates than other firs. Both have a symmetrical, pyramidlike appearance that makes pruning somewhat difficult. Great choices for a living Christmas tree.

Flax, New Zealand

3-9' • Sun or filtered sun

Large, swordlike purple red leaves spreading in a fan pattern make this a plant for special display. Grows in nearly every possible soil or exposure. On 'Atropurpureum' variety leaves often reach 9 feet long, but dwarf forms with 6-foot leaves are also available.

Juniper

1-20' • Sun or filtered sun

Picturesque in branch and trunk, these shrubs come in sizes and shapes to fit nearly any container need. One of the best is slow-growing, sage green *Juniperus chinensis* 'San Jose', which spreads 2 feet by 6 feet. Effective in large wooden containers, hollywood juniper, *J. c.* 'Torulosa', twists upright to 15 feet. *J. c.* 'Weaver' is compact, growing to 3 feet. Valued for hardiness in most climates, junipers can be pruned for shape easily.

Maple, Japanese

1–20' • Filtered sun or shade

Lacy, delicate tree has year-round interest—red leaf growth in spring, green foliage in summer turning to scarlet in autumn, and bare winter branch structure. To encourage healthy appearance, give maple ample water, periodic feeding, and shelter from heat and drying winds. Slow-growing—a tree can remain in a container for many years.

Norfolk Island Pine

2–15' • Sun or filtered sun

Suitable both indoors and out, this evergreen conifer (not a true pine) produces horizontal tiers of feathery growth. Needs large amounts of water in desert climates; protection from winter cold is a must. Feed two or three times during growing season with complete fertilizer. Easily propagated from a cutting of the growing tip.

Palms

3–20' • Filtered sun

Attractive leaves with a tropical look become doubly dramatic when a palm is containerized. For best effect, locate in a prominent spot—young palms prefer indoors, but others tolerate protected outdoor sites such as a shaded patio if temperatures are warm. Palms like ample moisture and frequent feedings. When repotting, select a pot only slightly larger than the previous one.

Here are some palms suitable for container living:

Chamaedorea seifrizii. Cluster palm of dense, compact growth to 10 feet; the feathery leaves have narrow leaflets.

Mediterranean fan palm. Hardiest of all palms, but growth can be slow in cold areas. Produces bluish green fan-shaped leaves, 2 to 3 feet across.

Parlor palm. This excellent indoor palm tolerates crowded conditions and poor light. Grows slowly to 3 to 4 feet. Effective when three or more plants are grouped in one large container.

Sentry palm. Arching, feathery leaves are 6 to 7 feet long. A great container choice—tolerates shade, will withstand neglect.

Philodendron

2–10' • Filtered sun

Recognized by their striking, glossy leaves, philodendrons fall into two groups: hardy, for outdoor use in mild climates, and tender, for indoor use.

Hardiest of the big-leafed outdoor varieties is *P. selloum;* it needs a large container, as it often reaches 8 to 10 feet. Give it a loose, well-drained soil and ample moisture and feeding.

For indoor philodendrons, see page 66. For split-leaf philodendron, see page 67.

Pine

5–30' • Sun

In large tubs or half barrels, pines make a striking addition to any garden. Planted in basic well-drained soil, they thrive in full sun. Once or twice a year, feed with complete fertilizer, but avoid fertilizers high in nitrogen. With proper care, many pines can last 10 years or more in containers. Some gardeners bring them indoors during the holidays for a "living" Christmas tree.

Here are five especially good pines for containers:

Bristlecone pine. Bushy and dense, with ground-sweeping branches. Slow growing to 20 feet.

Japanese black pine. Irregular, spreading growth makes it excellent for pruning, especially bonsai. Grows to 30 feet.

Japanese red pine. Often forms two trunks at soil line. Handsome and informal. Locate away from cold winds.

Mugho pine. Small, dense yet pleasing shape; height to 4 feet. Hardy, but suffers from drying in desert heat.

Shore pine. Symmetrical, narrow-crowned pine with dense foliage. Good choice for small gardens. Attractive at any height.

Podocarpus

3–40' • Sun or filtered sun

Suitable both indoors and out, these clean, pest-free trees have limber branches that can be espaliered. Fern pine (*P. gracilior*) has grayish green leaves; yew pine (*P. macrophyllus*) has broader, bright green leaves. Dependable and slow-growing.

Silverberry

5–15' • Sun

A perfect evergreen plant for portable screening because it is wind and heat resistant. Grayish green leaves have rusty dots that sparkle with reflected sunlight. Easy to prune into various shapes.

Spruce

5–30' • Filtered sun

Popular grown in a tub as a living Christmas tree. Dwarf varieties such as white spruce (*Picea glauca* 'Conica') with its soft, grayish green needles, are especially suited. Provide a cool location and ample water; shelter spruces from heat and drying winds.

Supported *on trellis, carefully pruned loquat appears as small tree form.*

Twisted, *irregular branching of Hollywood juniper fills empty corner with vertical growth. Pebbled container reflects seaside surroundings.*

Tubbed pyracanthas *positioned on both sides of house soften bare corner with espaliered, leafy growth.*

Mixed bouquets are garden spectaculars

These giant bouquets are surprisingly easy to create. All you need is a large container full of good potting soil (see page 24), an assortment of flowering plants, and enough know-how to keep them watered, fed, and groomed so they bloom heavily for a long time.

Half barrels, pots, tubs, or other containers that are at least 18 inches wide give the plants ample root space and provide the right scale for really dramatic combinations. Your bouquet can be a combination of just about anything—annuals, perennials, bulbs—as long as it grows well in your climate. Plan a specific color scheme following a suggestion on our chart, or just mix things up and wait for the surprises.

To get that bursting-at-the-seams look, cram the plants in much closer than you would in garden beds. For most combinations, 4 inches apart is about right. Forcing plants to compete for space produces some remarkable results—plants grow up and out like an arrangement of cut flowers in a vase. And there's less chance of color gaps if some plants fail to grow.

Give your mixed bouquets a good start by keeping them continuously moist and well fed; don't let them dry out during hot weather. A feeding of slow-release fertilizer at the time of planting should carry them through the season, or you can use a starter solution at the time of planting and then begin regular feeding every 7 to 10 days.

To encourage flower production over a long period, remove faded blossoms before they set seed.

Wire-frame basket *holds purple lobelia, red fibrous begonias, yellow and orange marigolds, white sweet alyssum, needlepoint ivy.*

Vivid *phlox, lobelia. Design: Michael Westgard.*

Portuguese wine barrels *hold marguerites, geraniums, petunias, marigolds, dusty miller, lobelia, viscaria. Dollies make them movable. Design: Michael Westgard.*

Roll-around planter *with pink geraniums, dwarf marguerites, blue and white petunias, dusty miller, yellow marigolds, lobelia. Design: Michael Westgard.*

Red *angelwing begonias with purple lobelia.*

Bright red geraniums, *yellow marigolds, purple lobelia massed in low aggregate planter. Design: W. David Poot.*

Mixed bouquets   53

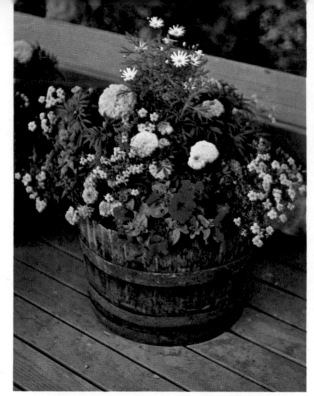

Trio *of favorites: red petunias, white daisies, yellow marigolds. Design: W. David Poot.*

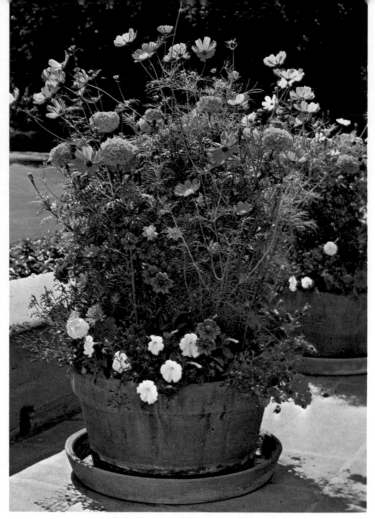

Colorful assortment *of flowering plants is easy to assemble. (See first combination on chart, next page.)*

Eye-catching bouquet *positioned near entry steps extends a friendly greeting. Design: R. David Adams.*

Identical pots *of marigolds, geraniums. Design: Michael Westgard.*

Our mixed bouquet planting chart gives you some specific color schemes indicating where to plant what in each container.

Along the edge	In between	In the center
Lobelia (dark blue) Petunias (red, white) Nasturtiums (orange, yellow)	Zinnias (orange yellow) Celosia (red, orange) Marigolds (yellow)	Cosmos (pink, red, white) Marigolds (gold) Salpiglossis (mixed)
Variegated ivy, trailing Lobelia (dark blue) Marigolds (single yellow)	African Daisy (orange) Marigolds (yellow) Geraniums (single white)	Marguerites (yellow)
Alyssum (white) Lobelia (soft blue)	Petunia (yellow)	Snapdragons (orange, rust)
Lotus berthelotii (silvery gray) Lobelia, trailing (blue)	Marigolds (yellow) Dusty Miller	Marigolds (yellow) Nicotiana (white)
Marigolds (orange, pale yellow)	Petunias (single white) Marigolds (yellow)	Cosmos (white)
Dwarf Morning Glory 'Royal Ensign' Alyssum (white) Lobelia (blue)	Petunias (white)	Zinnias (yellow)
Ageratum (blue)	*Phlox drummondii* (mixed pastel shades)	*Salvia farinacea* 'Blue Bedder' Marguerites (white)
Alyssum (white)	Dusty Miller Petunias (white) Celosia (yellow)	Geraniums (orange)
Petunias (dark blue, white)	Snapdragons (yellow)	Salpiglossis (mixed)
Ageratum (blue)	Bedding Dahlias (mixed orange, yellow, red, white) Cosmos (yellow)	Marguerites (yellow)
Campanula portenschlagiana (violet blue)	Fibrous Begonias (pink or white)	Impatiens (white)
Alyssum (white) Lobelia (soft blue)	Ornamental Basil 'Dark Opal' (purple leaves, pink flowers) Dusty Miller	Cosmos (white) Salpiglossis (mixed)

Edibles in containers

More and more gardeners who are becoming excited about growing food crops face the same obstacle: lack of suitable planting space. They know that to produce a good yield, most edible plants require sunlight, ample moisture and feeding, and *some* growing room. But what they don't realize is that many of the edibles—vegetables, herbs, and dwarf fruit trees—thrive in the confines of containers, taking up very little space at all.

Large wooden boxes, half barrels, pressed-pulp pots, and large clay pots all make practical containers deep enough for all but the largest vegetables. Smaller vegetables grow easily in hanging baskets, window boxes, or drainage tiles—just about anything that holds soil and drains freely. To make the most of their containers, some gardeners combine vegetables and flowers for a display that's both decorative and useful.

• **Planting.** Fill the containers with a porous, fast-draining soil. Use a commercial mix or try making your own (see page 24). In either case, a day or two before planting, add lime and superphosphate to correct acidity and guarantee that sufficient phosphorus will be available to the roots immediately. You can also try adding to the mix as much as one quarter soil from the garden; it will supply micronutrients not contained in the other ingredients.

To maintain steady growth, feed vegetables weekly with a complete fertilizer (fish emulsion is fine), or use a controlled-release fertilizer that provides nutrients for the entire growing season from a single application. Remember to check the soil for moisture each day—in extremely hot weather, containers may need watering at least that often.

Vegetables

Beans

Midspring–midsummer • 50–90 days • Warm-season crop

Limas and snap beans, green and yellow wax beans train up a trellis or grow in bush form. Sow seeds directly into containers—half barrels, pulp pots, large redwood boxes—and water often by soaking soil well.

Beets

After frost or in fall • 45–65 days • Cool-season crop

A redwood planter box with 12 inches of soil makes a compact, handy container for growing beets. For a heavy yield throughout the summer, sow seeds 3 inches apart at monthly intervals. Immature tops are tasty, too.

Carrots

Early spring or fall • 65–75 days • Cool-season crop

Almost any container 12 to 15 inches deep that drains well and can hold moist, porous soil can be used for growing carrots Try planting miniature or short varieties such as 'Tiny Sweet' every 2 weeks, keeping soil moist until leafy tops appear.

Chard

Early spring–late summer • 45–60 days • Perennial crop

"Decorative and edible" best describes Swiss chard. Hardy, red-stemmed 'Rhubarb', often planted with lettuce or spinach, mixes easily in containers of colorful annuals. To encourage continuous growth, harvest only outer leaves.

Cucumbers

Early summer–midsummer • 55–70 days • Warm-season crop

Save space and keep fruit off ground by tying vining cucumbers to a support—a fence post, chicken wire or wood frame, or a heavy twine netting. Or suspend such dwarf varieties as 'Little Minnie' and 'Patio Pick' in a hanging basket. Plant seeds in rich, fast-draining soil; thin seedlings to 10 inches apart. Lots of water and frequent feeding are essential.

Five-foot bamboo poles, *lashed together and strung with cotton or nylon cording, support container crops like pole beans, cucumbers, some squashes.*

Eggplant

Midspring–early summer • 65–80 days • Warm-season crop

Striking foliage and large purple fruit are spectacular in half barrels or large wooden tubs. In early spring, set out young plants—either purchased from nursery or sown indoors 8 weeks earlier. Water thoroughly, feed every 4 to 6 weeks.

Kale

Early spring–late summer • 60–70 days • Cool-season crop

The curly kales, especially bright-leafed flowering varieties such as 'Dwarf Blue Curled', are decorative container plants. Sow seeds directly into soil. To encourage continuous growth, harvest outside leaves. Serve raw in salads or cooked.

Lettuce

Early–late spring or fall • 40–80 days • Cool-season crop

Easy to grow and attractive in window boxes or clay, pulp, or other big pots. Try circling a bushy tomato plant with red leaf lettuce, or stagger Romaine and butter lettuce with green onions and radishes—all offer a handy supply of fresh salad ingredients. Sow seeds or set out transplants in rich, loose soil; water regularly and protect from hottest sun.

Onions, Green (Scallions)

Early spring or fall • 60–75 days • Cool-season crop

Seeds of small bunching onions or scallions sprout easily from seed in cool soil. 'Evergreen Bunching' and 'Beltsville Bunching' are suitable for containers if thinned 1 to 2 inches apart.

Peppers, Green and Red

Midspring–early summer • 60–80 days • Warm-season crop

Handsome bushes, decorative fruits, and sustained, heavy yield make peppers ideal for containers. Set out plants (started indoors 8 weeks earlier) in tubs or pots, spacing 18 inches apart. Feed twice after blooms set, water often.

Radishes

Early spring or fall • 20–50 days • Cool-season crop

This fast-growing root crop needs only 8 inches of soil to produce. Try combining radishes in a large wooden planter with other cool-weather vegetables—carrots, lettuce, beets. Sow seeds at 2-week intervals; avoid hot-weather harvests.

Squash, Summer

Early summer–midsummer • 50–60 days • Warm-season crop

Select high-yielding, fast-growing types of summer squash, such as 'Early Summer Crookneck' or 'Aristocrat' zucchini, for container life. Broad plants require heavy watering and fertilizing; constant picking prolongs the harvest period.

Tomatoes

Midspring–early summer • 55–90 days • Warm-season crop

If staked and supported, any type of tomato can be raised in a large, deep container. However, dwarf tomatoes and cherry or pear tomatoes are better adapted to pot or basket culture. Try suspending a pot of cascading tomatoes in a sunny patio—'Tiny Tim' and 'Atom' bear tasty, small fruit.

 Seeds are slow to sprout; set plants out in midspring, or start from seed indoors, 6 to 8 weeks earlier. Water growing plants often; fertilize monthly.

Wire cylinder *supports tomato vine, eliminates tying up, keeps fruit clean and within easy reach. Small root crops—carrots, radishes, scallions— easily grow around edges.*

Herbs

Basil, Sweet

12–24" • Annual • Sun or filtered sun

Shiny leaves have spicy, clovelike flavor that complements such foods as eggs, cheese, meats, and tomato dishes. Give it frequent watering to keep leaves succulent and a periodic pinching to encourage new growth and bushiness.

Chives

6–24" • Perennial • Sun or filtered sun

Round, hollow stems growing in grassy clumps from small bulbs have mild oniony flavor. This perennial herb—evergreen in mild areas, usually dormant in severe-winter areas—prefers rich, moist soil and occasional fertilizing, especially right after cutting. Clip top of stems for fresh chives as needed, or dry or freeze them for future use.

Dill

12–36" • Annual • Sun

Feathery light green leaves and small, pale yellow flower heads characterize this favorite herb. Grows best in full sun and well-drained soil. Use aromatic leaves and seeds in preparing fish, meat, and chicken dishes, sauces, and breads. Harvest ripe seeds just before they drop to ground; pick leaves when flowers first open and use fresh or dried.

How to dry herbs

If you grow more herbs than you can use right away, here's how to dry and store them.

The best time to harvest sprigs is when plants have a lot of foliage, preferably when the flowers first open—the flavoring oils are most concentrated then. If you don't cut heavily, most herbs will produce a second or third large harvest by fall.

Hang herbs in a dry, well-ventilated, moderately warm place away from direct sunlight. Tie them in small bunches so they'll dry quickly and retain color and fragrance. In 3 to 7 days herbs will be dry enough to crumble; store airtight in a dark place. Use them for cooking, sachets, pillows, and gifts.

Garlic

6–36" • Perennial bulb • Sun

Familiar garlic bulblets ("cloves") grow from mother bulbs or sets, sold at many nurseries and seed stores. Plant individually in rich, well-drained soil. When leafy stem tops begin to droop, harvest bulbs by digging or pulling them up; store in a dry, airy place.

Mint

6–36" • Perennial • Filtered sun or shade

Orange, golden apple, spearmint, and peppermint-flavored leaves grow on bushy plants that spread rapidly. They prefer a light, rich soil and ample watering. Use for lamb, cold drinks, tea, jelly, and for garnishing.

Oregano

12–40" • Perennial • Sun

Fresh or dried, oregano leaves are one of the distinct flavors of Mexican and Italian cooking. Shrubby, round-leafed plant is dependable, growing best in well-drained soil with ample moisture. To encourage bushiness and full foliage, cut back flowering plant occasionally.

Parsley

6–12" • Biennial • Filtered sun or shade

Decorative, fernlike foliage, used fresh as a garnish and fresh or dried in many different dishes, can be picked the year around. In containers, it's useful as a leafy border with colorful annuals. Harvest before flower spikes appear—from then on, leaves taste bitter.

Rosemary

6–24" • Perennial • Sun

Low-growing, twisting 'Prostratus' variety, with glossy needlelike foliage, spills tiny lavender blue flowers over container's edge. Hardy herb tolerates hot sun. Use fresh or dried leaves to season meat and vegetable dishes and in teas.

Sage

12–36" • Perennial • Sun

Familiar garden sage has narrow gray leaves and spikes of fragrant violet flowers. Thrives in full sun with little watering. Cut back stems and fertilize after blooming. Use fresh or dried leaves with lamb, stuffings, poultry, and cheese dishes.

Savory, Summer

6–18" • Annual • Sun

Narrow, aromatic leaves have a delicate peppery flavoring, good either fresh or dry as a mild seasoning for meat, fish, eggs, soups, and salad dressings. Sow seeds directly in container in light, rich soil; locate in full sun, water occasionally.

Tarragon

12–24" • Perennial • Sun or filtered sun

Woody, spreading branches bear pointed, quite aromatic dark leaves. Thrives in rich, well-drained soil; needs some protection from hottest sun. Use anise-flavored fresh or dried leaves in vinegars or to season fish, eggs, and salads.

Thyme

2–12" • Perennial • Sun

Shrubby common thyme, planted in fairly dry, porous soil, quickly spreads to 2 feet wide if not pruned regularly. Fresh or dried leaves have strong aromatic flavor useful in meat, vegetable, and poultry dishes.

Don't hesitate to try other herbs that appeal to you. Near an entry or an open window, delightfully fragrant ones such as lemon balm, chamomile, lavender, and lemon verbena are especially nice.

Fruit

Citrus, dwarf varieties

3–9' • Sun

Glossy evergreen foliage, fragrant blossoms, and colorful fruit characterize dwarf citrus trees. In mild-winter areas, containers can be left outdoors all year; elsewhere, move indoors during winter and place in a cool, well-lighted room or basement.

In hot weather, daily watering may be necessary; a

2-inch pebble mulch helps to conserve moisture. Use a high-nitrogen (citrus) fertilizer in late winter, in June, and again in August.

Here are some dwarf varieties to try:

Kumquat. 'Nagami', 3 to 4 feet, bears 1-inch orange fruit in autumn.

Lemon. 'Eureka', the standard lemon, bears all year; 'Meyer', tangy and juicy, bears early.

Lime. 'Bearss' is thorny, bears seedless lemon-size fruit; 'Mexican' is a typical small green lime.

Mandarin orange. 'Dancy' produces traditional Christmas fruit. 'Kinnow' ripens in spring, a good citrus for any climate.

Orange. 'Robertson', good in warm interiors, bears heavily in winter; 'Shamouti', beautiful in form and foliage, bears in spring.

Tangelo. Red-pulped fruit similar to grapefruit; 'Sampson' hybrid is good for juice and marmalades.

Fruit Trees, dwarf varieties

3–10' • Sun

Edible fruit follows cheery spring blossoms on dwarf trees. Peach, apricot, apple, and pear are suited for large tubs; well-drained soil and ample watering are essential. Your nurseryman can help you select a variety best suited for your climate and location.

Deep *ceramic planter holds fruit-laden mandarin orange.*

Sunny *rooftop garden has pots of vegetables, herbs.*

Guava

3–10' • Sun

Subtropical pineapple guava *(Feijoa sellowiana)* bears bland, pineapple-flavored fruit in autumn. Strawberry guava *(Psidium cattleianum)* has attractive bark and glossy golden leaves, bears sweet-tart red fruit in autumn and winter. Useful as a portable screen; also a fine bonsai subject.

Loquat

4–15' • Sun or filtered sun

Large, handsome leathery leaves with sweet, aromatic orange fruit make this evergreen a good tubbed tree for deck or patio. Thrives in moist soil in sun or partial shade.

Pomegranate

3–10' • Sun

Showy, orange-red spring flowers are followed by burnished red fruits and golden leaves in autumn. Will tolerate extreme heat and poor soil; needs sun for fruit production. 'Wonderful', the best-known variety, has excellent fruit. 'Nana' is a dense 3-foot dwarf, suitable for bonsai.

Midget *corn thrives in half barrel on sunny patio.*

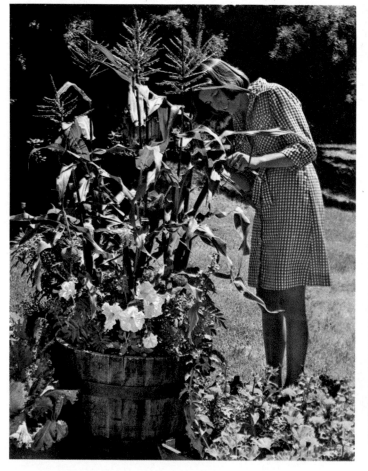

Strawberries

2–8' • Sun

Large-fruited 'Sequoia', 'Northwest', or 'Lassen' varieties are hardy and delicious. Use any large container—strawberry planter, long redwood box, half barrel, or even a large washtub with drainage holes. Locate in full sun in rich, well-drained soil; fertilize when growth begins and after first crop.

Daily *harvest of ripe cherry tomatoes.*

Potpourri *of herb-filled containers.*

Stage a flower show with bulbs

Bulbs and bulblike plants are naturals for container life. They're easy to grow, and the portability provided by containers gives you color where you want it, both indoors and out. By selecting species and varieties according to their bloom period, you can enjoy a succession of bulb color throughout the year.

With little more than an occasional repotting or refurbishing, bulbs such as amaryllis, canna, and clivia can remain containerized for several years. Others, less durable—crocus, daffodils, Dutch iris, hyacinths, and tulips—are usually grown in containers for one season and then either planted in garden beds or discarded.

We use the term *bulb* to include not only true bulbs but corms, tubers, rhizomes, and tuberous roots as well. These plants all have one thing in common: their bulbs or bulblike structures store food. The plant draws on these reserves to start active growth after its season of dormancy. This food is manufactured in the leaves, so if you're planning to keep a bulb for future bloom, let the leaves remain on the plant to ripen and dry naturally. The longer the leaves remain on the plant, the bigger the bulb will be to produce next year's flowers.

● **Bulb culture.** Always try to buy No. 1 bulbs. In most cases, the sooner you plant them after they become available, the better (that means in late fall for spring bloom, in winter for summer and fall bloom). Most bulbs grow well in loose, fibrous planting mix containing equal parts of soil, coarse sand, and organic matter such as peat moss, leaf mold, or ground bark. Plant large bulbs so the tips are level with the surface of the soil; small ones should be slightly under the surface.

Water the containers thoroughly, filling them to the rim two or three times to be sure the mix is wet throughout. Place them in a cool, dark place while the roots are forming—a shaded spot on the north side of the house or under a tree will keep the soil in pots cool and prevent premature sprouting. Where the winters are extremely warm, you will need further insulation to keep bulbs cool: in a trench, place the containers on a layer of sand or gravel and cover them with 3 to 4 inches of moist peat moss, wood shavings, sawdust, or sand. Or set them in a frame deep enough to accommodate the layer of mulch.

After about 8 weeks, lift a few pots and see if roots are showing in the drainage hole or if leaf tips have poked through the surface. If so, place the containers in a light spot while the top growth develops. When tops are green, move containers into the sun to bloom.

Amaryllis (Naked Lady)

1–3' • Late summer bloom • Sun

Fragrant, trumpet-shaped flowers in red, pink, or green-tinged white bloom on leafless 3-foot stems. In late autumn, plant bulbs in rich, sandy soil, setting top of bulb slightly above dirt surface. Drought-resistant and long-blooming, amaryllis are a traditional companion to soft-blue agapanthus.

Anemone

6–14" • Spring bloom • Sun

Showy, poppylike flowers bloom in single or mixed. colors of red, violet, blue, or white. In October or November, set out presoaked tubers, planting them 1 to 2 inches deep in rich, well-drained soil. The most commonly grown species, *A. coronaria,* is best suited to container life.

Begonia, Tuberous

6–30" • Summer bloom • Filtered sun

Choose from many flower forms and colors, including spectacular upright *B. tuberhybrida* or cascading *B. t. 'Pendula'*. In January or February, when pink buds appear on tubers, plant them in coarse leaf mold. Later, when plants are 3 inches high, transplant to pots or wooden boxes—many gardeners favor cedar or redwood containers because they hold moisture best. Flowers bloom throughout summer in rich reds, pinks, and yellows, and in white. Locate in partial shade and keep soil moist.

Winter-blooming *elatior begonias near sunny window.*

Bluebells, see Scilla

Canna, Pfitzer Dwarf

1–3' • Summer bloom • Sun

Large wooden planters of single-colored canna add a tropical look to any midsummer garden. Canna resembles a banana or ti plant; it likes rich, moist soil and warm climates. Flowers appear in reds, oranges, and white.

Clivia, see Kaffir Lily

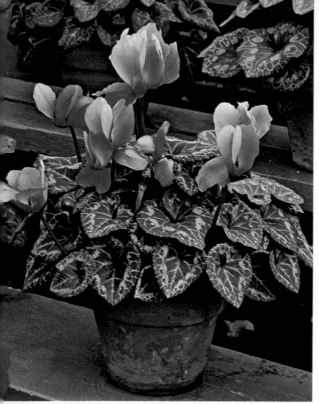

Vivid *cyclamen are indoor-outdoor favorites.*

Crocus
4-10" • Autumn, winter, spring bloom • Sun

Mass these hardy corms in boxes or pots, or scatter a few at the base of a spring-flowering tree or shrub. Colorful little cups of vivid yellow, violet, or white appear above grasslike clumps of leaves. Adapted to sun or filtered shade.

Steps of deck *are lined with potted lemon yellow daffodils.*

A dozen *Dutch hyacinths in each pot.*

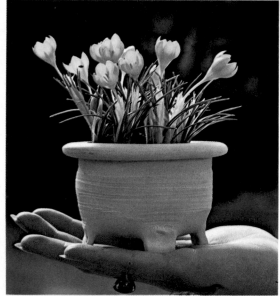

Crocus ancyrensis *in natural porcelain pot.*

Cyclamen

6–10" • Autumn, winter, spring bloom • Shade

Large pink, white, red, or rose-colored flowers appear high above rounded, often variegated leaves. Plant tubers in rich, porous soil during their dormant period (June to August); the top half should be visible above soil surface. Locate in a somewhat shady area.

Daffodil (Narcissus)

8–24" • Winter, spring bloom • Sun

Easiest to grow and most popular of all the bulbs. In single or bicolored combinations of yellow, orange, and cream, daffodils are consistently good performers. For a long season of color (December to April), plant early and late varieties in October or November. In wooden boxes or terra cotta pots, they give sparkle to a terrace or patio, on steps, or near entry. Keep well watered until leaves turn yellow.

Dahlia

1–3' • Summer bloom • Sun

Compact dwarf dahlias of ball, pompon, and collarette types, valued for their varied flower forms and colors, are best suited for display in containers. Plant tubers in rich, sandy soil about 3 inches deep and keep moist throughout the growing season.

Freesia

12–18" • Spring bloom • Sun

Blooming on slender 18-inch stems, sweet-scented freesias have large single or bicolored flowers in white, orange, pink, or purple. In each pot plant several corms of the same color, setting them 2 inches deep. In cold climates, grow indoors or in coldframes until frosts are past.

Hyacinth

8–18" • Spring bloom • Sun

Size of flower spike is directly related to size of bulb. Flowers are waxy, bell-shaped, and fragrant in white and cream through shades of red, purple, and blue. Excellent in cold-winter areas, they may also be grown indoors in water in a special hyacinth glass. Plant bulbs in fall for spring bloom. For an effective display, mass in pots under a shading tree.

Iris

1–4' • Spring, summer bloom • Sun

All but the very tallest iris make showy, graceful additions to a container garden. Bulbous iris such as Dutch, English, and Wedgwood are especially adaptable to containers, as are dwarf and miniature varieties of rhizomatous iris. In late autumn, plant six or eight bulbs in a 6-inch pot, watering lightly until roots form. Flowers appear in full color range except green and true red.

Kaffir Lily (Clivia)

1–2' • Winter, spring bloom • Filtered sun

Clusters of funnel-shaped orange blooms rise above clumps of wide, dark green leaves in winter or early spring. These are ideal for containers because they flourish when roots are crowded. Plant in rich soil with top half of tuber exposed. Plants like constant moisture and shade most of the day.

Lily

1–5' • Summer bloom • Filtered sun

For late spring and summer color in containers, lilies are unsurpassed. For smaller kinds, place one bulb in a deep 5-inch pot; for larger types, put several bulbs in a larger box or tub. In general, lilies require: 1) a planting mix of sand, soil, and peat in equal parts; 2) ample moisture throughout the year; and 3) shade at the roots and filtered sun for blooming tops. Superb container varieties include 'Enchantment' (with red orange flowers), *Lilium henryi* hybrids, *L. longiflorum* and hybrids, and *L. speciosum* and hybrids.

Naked Lady, see Amaryllis

Narcissus, see Daffodils

Nerine

1–2' • Autumn bloom • Sun

Iridescent, wispy pink or scarlet flowers with crinkly petals bloom on 1 to 2-foot stems in autumn. Just as bulbs begin to grow (August to October), plant one in a 4-inch pot or three in a 6-inch pot, exposing the top half of each bulb above the soil surface. Like clivia, nerine flowers best when roots are crowded.

Ranunculus

18–24" • Spring, summer bloom • Sun

Resembling jumbo-size single or double buttercups, ranunculus come in a vivid array of yellow, orange, pink, red, cream, and white tufted flowers. Soak the bone-hard, clawlike tubers in water for several hours, then start them in flats of moist sand or perlite. When tops of plants are 3 inches high, set three plants in a 7-inch pot or plant a dozen or more in a tub or large box. Or plant tubers directly in pots, about 1 inch below the soil surface. Water regularly and feed with a complete fertilizer once a month.

Scilla (Bluebell)

4–12" • Spring or autumn bloom • Sun

Accent a spring garden of golden daffodils or pure white snowdrops with containers of sparkling bluebells. These bell-shaped flowers on leafless stalks appear in brilliant blue, pink, purple, or white. Plant in autumn, usually six bulbs to a 6-inch pot; only one large bulb is needed when you plant the foot-tall Peruvian variety. Scilla needs lots of moisture.

Tulip

6–24" • Spring bloom • Sun

Stately and formal, dainty and whimsical, or bordering on bizarre—depending on the kind—most tulips display well in containers. Set bulbs out in rich, sandy soil in October or November (but postpone planting if weather is still warm); tips should be level with or just under the soil surface. Tulips like open sky and sun for a good part of the day but appreciate light shade in the spring months to help prolong flowering. Blooms are single or bicolored—often striped or banded—in nearly all shades of red, yellow, orange, purple, and white.

Plants for small garden pools

Most water gardeners prefer to grow their pool plants in containers, both for easy access to the plants and to make pool maintenance easier. When you think of pool plants, you think of water lilies. Hardy, dependable water plants, they are available in an extraordinary range of sizes and shapes, in shades from white to yellow to rose and deep red. But specialists also sell many other bog or aquatic plants that send up their leaves or blooms to float on the water's surface.

Our list describes some of the water plants best adapted to the limited depth of small pools. At nurseries specializing in pool plants, you'll find many additional choices.

Use ordinary garden soil for planting, even if it's heavy clay. Plastic, wooden, or clay containers are all satisfactory, but avoid redwood as it colors the water. Place bog plants near the surface of the water, no deeper than 1 or 2 inches; aquatics should be set deep, usually with the top of the soil between 6 and 8 inches below the surface, but up to 12 inches for larger lilies.

Most water plants prefer full sun, although in the desert they may need some shade in the afternoon. Feeding is seldom necessary except with water lilies, which require special fertilizers.

Arrowhead

1–4' • Sun

Arching, grasslike leaves are dark green, handsome. May produce small white flowers if stems rise high out of water. An oxygenating plant, arrowhead enjoys ample sunlight and water depth of 12 to 14 inches.

A barrelful

Here's how to make a summer day seem a little cooler: create a water garden in a wooden barrel. You'll need an empty half barrel (25 gallons), a few plants, maybe a goldfish or two, and a little water.

First, fill the half barrel with water and stir in about a cupful of lime to neutralize the inside. Let it sit for a few days; then empty it and move it to its permanent location. (Give that location plenty of thought—a 25-gallon half barrel full of water weighs about 200 pounds.) You might try a corner of your garden if there is water seepage from the barrel.

Tub water gardens usually are planted with bog or aquatic plants. Our illustration shows water lily *(Nymphaea)*, arrowhead *(Sagittaria latifolia)*, dwarf papyrus *(Cyperus haspan)*, and water lettuce *(Pistia stratiotes)*. Place bog plants near the surface of the water, no deeper than 1 or 2 inches. Aquatics can be planted deep—between 6 and 12 inches, depending on the variety.

Once a year, drain and scrub the barrel thoroughly. Meanwhile, put a solitary goldfish to work—he'll help keep it clean by eating mosquito larvae that hatch.

Horsetail

1–4' • Sun

Bright green, rushlike hollow stems with distinctive black joints characterize horsetail. A vigorous grower, horsetail should be planted in a partially submerged pot in full sun.

Japanese Iris

2–3' • Filtered sun

Pastel summer blooms—pinks to purples and white—and graceful, sword-shaped foliage enhance any garden pool. After planting rhizomes 2 inches deep in potting mix, submerge pot halfway to the rim in water.

Lotus

2–6' • Sun

Beautiful, fragrant blooms 4 to 10 inches wide, usually pink but often combinations of red and white, rise above water surface with large leaves. The ornamental woody fruits are useful in dried arrangements. Plant in spring in 12-inch-deep container; place so soil surface is 8 to 12 inches under water. In winter, protect from freezing by covering pool or storing roots.

Papyrus, Dwarf

2–6' • Sun

Give garden ponds a delicate Oriental accent with dwarf papyrus reeds. Foot-long tufts of narrow flower stalks top its 18-inch stems. Root in several inches of water.

Umbrella Plant

2–4' • Sun

Dwarf form, *Cyperus alternifolius* 'Nanus', has spreading leaves like the ribs of an umbrella. Thrives in shallow water. In cold-winter areas, move plant indoors and locate in a well-lighted room.

Water Hyacinth

6–36" • Sun or filtered sun

Hollow-stemmed type, *Eichhornia crassipes*, bears violet flowers with yellow eyes; *E. azurea* has purple to blue blooms. Both have floating or submerged leaves and feathery roots; need warmth to flower profusely.

Water Lily

8–30" • Sun or filtered sun

Select either hardy lilies to stay in pool all winter, or tropical lilies, which must be stored and replanted each year in all but the mildest climates. Rounded leaves, deeply notched at the base, float on water's surface around showy flowers.

Nymphaea odorata and *N. tetragona* are hardy varieties producing 3 to 5-inch flowers that bloom in daytime. Generally, each lily plant needs about 4 square feet of water surface.

In spring, set out rootstock just beneath the soil surface in plastic or wooden boxes about 8 inches deep. Dwarf kinds grow in 4 to 8 inches of water.

Water Poppy

1–2' • Sun

Three-petaled flowers resembling miniature California poppies are yellow with purple stamens. Broad leaves float on surface of water. Locate pots in sunny pool in 2 feet of water.

Indoor favorites

Listed here are the house plants found to be the most popular and reliable of the hundreds grown indoors. For a more complete listing, refer to the *Sunset* book *How to Grow House Plants.* Other species listed throughout this book, though not considered house plants, can be rotated between indoors and out—some for a brief period, others for an entire season. Plants kept indoors in containers require little more care than their counterparts grown outside. Strong, bright light (no scorching sun), ample watering and feeding, and an occasional misting to help raise humidity will keep plants healthy. Commercial potting soil, packaged and sold in varying sizes, is the most efficient planting medium for most varieties.

African Violet

4–8" • Year-round bloom • Strong sunless light

Fuzzy, heart-shaped leaves growing in rosettes produce clusters of colorful flowers—solid or variegated in purple, violet, pink, cerise, and white. High humidity, sufficient, indirect light, and slightly crowded roots in an acidic soil mix are essential for healthy growth. (Commercial African violet potting mix is available at most nurseries.) When watering, use warm water and avoid splashing on leaves or crown.

Aralia, Threadleaf False

1–4' • Moderate sunless light

A prominent spot such as a well-lighted hall or entry is ideal for displaying a threadleaf false aralia. Its narrow, dark green leaves are divided into lacy, fanlike clusters high atop stems. With the right conditions— high humidity, ample light, and monthly feeding— it can take on treelike proportions. Needs well-drained soil; be careful not to overwater.

Chinese Evergreen

8–30" • Moderate sunless light

Deep green, blotched leaves with contrasting veins and small, whitish flowers resembling callas characterize Chinese evergreen. Hardy, able to withstand abuse; one of the best plants for poorly lighted spots.

Dieffenbachia

1-6' • Moderate sunless light

Evergreen foliage plant with large, pointed variegated leaves; colors vary from dark green to chartreuse to white. Enjoys average house temperatures and humidity—can be summered outdoors on sheltered patio. Its nickname, "dumb cane," refers to the fact that the acrid sap in leaves will burn the mouth and may paralyze vocal cords.

Ficus Benjamina (Weeping Fig)

1-25' • Strong sunless light

Delicate appearance of the weeping fig—leathery, shiny green leaves suspended from drooping branches—makes it an indoor favorite among container gardeners. Vigorous grower, often reaching 8 to 12 feet, sometimes taller. Water thoroughly but infrequently, allowing soil to dry out between waterings. Can be summered outdoors in wind-protected areas where there is little direct sun.

Grape Ivy

1-6' • Moderate sunless light

This easy-to-grow climber can be trained upright on a trellis or stake or left to cascade over pot's edge. Three-sectioned leaves are dark glossy green and sharply toothed. Because of its tolerance for poor light and its undemanding nature, grape ivy is suited to almost any indoor location.

Ivy

1-5' • Moderate sunless light

Foliage is the word—leaves are large or small, green or variegated, heart-shaped or deep-lobed. Various kinds are suitable for containers from small ceramic pots to large wooden planters. Ivies enjoy cool temperatures and moist soil; will tolerate poor light. Try training ivy on a stake, wire frame, or trellis, or prune to shape for informal topiary as a ball, cone, or pyramid.

Orchids

6-30" • Strong sunless light

Orchids are either epiphytic (growing natively in tree branches and deriving nutrients from air and moisture) or terrestrial (growing natively in moist, humus-rich soil). For proper growth, they require special treatment—a planting mix of osmunda fiber, *hapuu* (tree fern fiber), or a commercial orchid mix; high light intensity (an east window behind sheer curtains is ideal); and high humidity.

Moisture is important, but overwatering will rot orchids. When soil looks dry and pot feels light when lifted, the plant needs water. The best time to repot—usually every 2 years—is shortly after flowering, when new roots start to grow.

Here is a list of easily grown orchids most favored for their bloom:

Cattleya. Best-known type; one to four blooms per stem, may flower twice a year.

Cypripedium. Elegant, glossy lady's slipper orchid, blooms in May and June.

Epidendrum. Easiest to grow, bears clusters of miniature orchids on arching stems.

Oncidium. Long, arching sprays of blossoms make excellent cut flowers; usually blooms in yellow.

Odontoglossum. Includes the striped tiger orchid and the fragrant lily-of-the-valley orchid.

Parlor Palm

1-4' • Moderate sunless light

Single-stemmed feathery tree, slow-growing to 4 feet, is best palm for indoors. Locate almost anywhere; tolerates crowding and poor light, but needs repotting every 2 or 3 years. Effective when planted three or more in a large container. (For outdoor palms, see page 50.)

Philodendron

1-6' • Moderate sunless light

Known for its attractive, leathery leaves in many sizes and shapes, a potted philodendron is a tough, durable indoor plant. Growing upright or vining, plants need support, good light, and ample water. Common *P. oxycardium* can be trained to frame a window on totem, trellis, or string; lobed, 10-inch leaves of *P. panduraeforme* grow on sturdy stems sometimes up to 6 feet.

Piggyback

6-24" • Strong sunless light

Name comes from its unusual appearance—tiny new plantlets sprout up on top of mature ones. Heart-shaped leaves are bright green and fuzzy with sharply toothed edges. Plenty of water and cool temperatures are important, and strong indirect light is needed for healthy growth.

Schefflera

1-15' • Strong sunless light

Indoor/outdoor foliage plant, often reaching 10 feet or more, needs ample room to show off its umbrellalike silhouette. Shiny oval leaflets, clustered 7 to 16 per group, stand away from plant on long sturdy stems. Care includes heavy watering and feeding, occasional pruning for shape. Effective in natural wood containers such as rough-sawn redwood or in old oak half barrels or tubs.

Split-leaf Philodendron

1–8' • Moderate sunless light

Favorite potted plant grows quite large with huge, dark green leaves deeply cut and perforated. Easily grown indoors and out; requires warm temperatures, high humidity, ample watering, and support for winding branches. To maintain glossy look, wash leaves occasionally with mild soap and water.

Table-top trio *of African violet favorites.*

Indoor assortment *trails from shelves in kitchen window.*

Leafy *grape ivy adorns bookcase shelf.*

Ficus benjamina *thrives in indoor/outdoor location. (Instructions for building container are on page 37.)*

Swedish Ivy

1-4' • Moderate sunless light

Fast-growing trailer with thick, almost succulent leaves and tiny flower spikes is attractive cascading over pot's edge or suspended from ceiling in a hanging planter. Likes humidity, lots of moisture; will tolerate poor light.

Wandering Jew

1-5' • Strong sunless light

Vigorous, fleshy vine has variegated leaves—purple, green, pale yellow, most with contrasting white veins. Needs to be hung from ceiling or beam—cascading stems may reach 4 to 5 feet. For intense leaf color, locate plant in well-lighted area away from direct sunlight; water frequently and mist occasionally.

Wandering Jew *cascades over table's edge.*

Weeping Fig, see Ficus Benjamina

Bonsai—a distinctive specialty

Almost any kind of woody plant material can be made into an attractive bonsai specimen. Of course, certain plants lend themselves better than others to certain treatments or styles, and some plants just don't take kindly to being confined in containers.

A few favorites of bonsai growers are listed here, but don't be timid about experimenting with others. Though only a few trees—pines, oaks, and maples—are classical choices, there is no reason why others can't be cultivated in this manner. Even herbs such as oregano and rosemary make handsome bonsai subjects.

For more information about bonsai and its techniques, refer to the Sunset book *Bonsai, Culture and Care of Miniature Trees.*

• **Planting a bonsai.** Any simple container that fits the character of the plant and doesn't detract from it is suitable for growing a bonsai. However, the classical Japanese bonsai pots seem most appropriate. Import stores and Oriental specialty shops usually have a good selection; some nurseries and garden centers also carry them.

Though bonsai fanciers all have their favorite formulas for planting mix, a basic mix combines equal parts of sand (river or quarry—not beach), leaf mold, and soil. Position the plant firmly in the mix; water thoroughly but gently. Trim excess branches, but leave major pruning until the plant is established. Do not fertilize for at least 4 or 5 weeks.

• **Pruning and training.** Wiring and bending of branches is best done in the spring when the wood is pliable. Use regular plastic or fabric-covered house wire (No. 10 or 20 size). Start wiring at the lowest point on the tree. Winding around the branch, keep the turns about ¼ inch apart and the wire snug but not tight against the wood. Secure the stub end of wire against the wood. Gently bend the branch in a wide radius, keeping in mind the general form you wish to create. Make bends gradual, avoiding any sharp angles or corners.

A bonsai specimen usually requires only one heavy branch pruning in its life—that one is to establish its basic form. From then on, shaping is done by nipping or pinching back new growth.

Azalea, Kurume
Compact twiggy plant, densely foliaged and growing in mounds, with profuse bloom of small flowers.

Camellia Sasanqua
The bushy or spreading habits are easily controlled by pruning. Numerous autumn and winter blooms.

Cotoneaster
Prune to enhance the twisted, prostrate branch habits. Red berries follow white flowers.

False Cypress, dwarf forms
Some of these evergreens (such as 'Squarrosa Minima') are compact little trees; others have curving or twisted branches that train easily. Prefers a sunny location.

Ginkgo Biloba
Graceful deciduous tree with airy, fan-shaped leaves that turn buttery yellow in autumn.

Juniper, Sargent
A classic bonsai plant valued for its picturesque form and feathery gray green foliage. Other prostrate kinds such as *J. conferta* also adapt to bonsai.

Maple
Trident maple*(Acer buergerianum)* has round crown of glossy leaves that turn red and gold in autumn. The Japanese maple *(A. palmatum)* and its varieties have year-round beauty. (See page 50).

Pine
Lacebark pine *(Pinus bungeana)* has flaking gray bark that reveals creamy branches and trunk. Jeffrey pine *(P.*

jeffreyi) has silver gray bark and blue foliage. Japanese black pine *(P. thunbergiana),* hardy and handsome, can be pruned into various shapes.

Pomegranate, Dwarf
Small red fruits follow orange red blossoms on dense little shrub *(Punica granatum* 'Nana') when it is only a foot tall.

Quince, Flowering
White or pink flowers of 'Contorta' bloom on twisted branches before leaves unfold. Adapts easily to wiring and training into interesting shapes.

Zelkova Serrata
Smooth gray bark combines with attractive elmlike foliage that turns to yellow and dark red in autumn.

Chinese wisteria, *25 years old, in full bloom.*

Exposed roots *of bonsai maple add interest, beauty.*

Ezo spruce *grows clinging to rocks.*

Group planting *of Japanese maples (Acer palmatum) makes miniature forest just 19 inches high.*

Bonsai   69

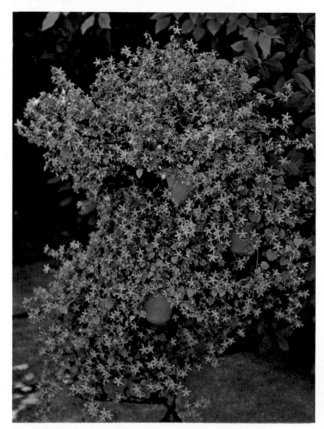

Asparagus fern *with bushy, needlelike foliage is dependable choice for most locations.*

These plants like to hang

The most popular plants for hanging containers have long, trailing stems that form a graceful cascade of flowers or foliage. The plants listed here fall into that category. But don't hesitate to try other plants in hanging containers if it strikes your fancy. Bulbs, a bonsai specimen, a mixed bouquet of small bedding plants, herbs, or other favorites may take on added importance when viewed at eye level.

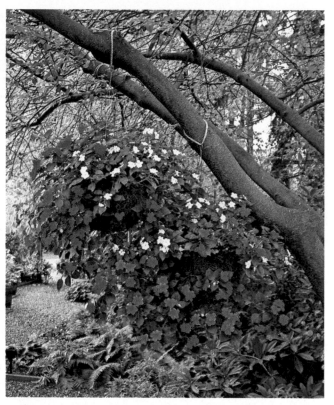

Under *shading tree, impatiens flourish, producing new flowers from planting until frost.*

Easy-to-grow *kangaroo treebine (Cissus antarctica).*

Spiral *wrought iron stand holds pots of trailing campanula. Star-shaped flowers are long-lasting, have excellent color.*

The basic techniques of gardening on the ground apply to gardening in the air, with one added consideration—the strength and location of the support structure. Take care to choose one that is strong enough to support the weight of your container filled with soil (a 12-inch wooden box or basket can weigh as much as 30 pounds—and even more after it has been watered). Choose a location that provides the right amount of sun or shade for your plant; avoid spots that are exposed to reflected heat or strong drying winds.

For information about containers and hangers, see pages 20-21.

Asparagus Fern

2-6′ • Filtered sun

Arching stems of coarse, needlelike foliage and seasonal scarlet berries characterize 'Sprenger' variety. Ideal for hanging containers, both indoors and out. Looks greenest when given partial shade and ample water.

Begonia, Tuberous

6-18″ • Filtered sun

Summer-blooming 'Pendula' variety, with sprays of vivid or pastel-colored flowers, has a trailing habit perfect for hanging containers. Locate in partial shade away from drying winds; keep soil moist but not soggy. See also page 61.

Campanula (Italian Bellflower)

1-2′ • Filtered sun

Clusters of trailing bellflowers are excellent for color in summer and autumn. Vinelike stems of *C. isophylla* produce blue, star-shaped flowers; *C. i.* 'Alba' has larger, white blooms. Effective by itself or in mixed baskets with other hanging plants such as fuchsias or petunias.

Donkey Tail Sedum

3-5′ • Filtered sun

Overlapping, fleshy, gray green leaves give a braided, ropelike appearance to this unique indoor/outdoor plant. Tails often cascade 3 feet or more when kept out of winds and traffic. It needs shade during some of the day, plenty of water, and fertilizing two or three times a year. Leaves can easily be rooted for new plants.

Fuchsia

1-2′ • Filtered sun

Select pendulous, free-flowering *F. hybrida* varieties to hang from a shading tree or under house eaves or protected patio overhangs. If given ample water and regular feedings of complete fertilizer, fuchsias have a long blooming period—early spring until frost. See also page 45.

Geranium, Ivy

1-3′ • Full sun

Trailing branches of glossy green, ivylike leaves surround blooms of white, red, pink, rose, and lavender flowers. Plant requires sun to develop intense color and enjoys lots of water, especially in warm weather. Other good choices for hangers include peppermint geranium, some fancy-leafed varieties, and trailing forms of Martha Washington geraniums.

Italian Bellflower, see Campanula

Ivy

1-4′ • Filtered sun

A cool, well-lit spot under a porch overhang or a shading tree is perfect for displaying baskets of trailing ivy. Choose from such tidy, small-leafed varieties as popular 'Hahn's Self Branching'. Pointed green or variegated foliage offers dependable year-round greenery. See also page 76.

Lobelia, Trailing

6-18″ • Filtered sun

Several plants in a 6-inch hanging pot will have lobelia's tiny-leafed, miniature blue flowers spilling over the edge. 'Sapphire,' with its deep blue flowers and white centers, and light blue 'Hamburgia' are good trailing choices. Plant in rich, well-drained soil; keep moist and well fertilized.

Your garden goes airborne *when you suspend plants from balcony ceilings, overhangs. Trailing plants screen out unwanted views.*

Lotus Berthelotii (Parrot's Beak)

2-3' • Filtered sun

Thickly covered silvery foliage produces scarlet blooms in midsummer. Plant does best in protected areas when kept well watered and fed. To encourage bushiness, cut back main stems occasionally.

Petunia, Cascade

12-28" • Sun

Single ruffled, sometimes striped flowers in vivid and pastel colors bloom on arching stems throughout spring and summer. For a massive display, use three plants to a 9-inch hanging pot; or mix cascading petunias with other colorful trailers such as lobelia or campanula. Water often and apply fertilizer monthly.

Ferns for indoors and out

Ferns are grown for the beauty of their foliage, from the delicate tracery of the maidenhair to the dramatic, graceful fronds of the sturdy tree fern. House plant fanciers always include several ferns in their collection, displaying both upright and trailing varieties. Outdoors, these handsome plants offer a striking, often tropical accent to a patio or garden.

Shade or filtered sunlight seems to suit ferns best. If they reside in the house, place them where they get good *bright* light but not direct sunlight. To help create the humid atmosphere they prefer, mist often and keep the soil moist but not soggy. During the growing season, ferns benefit from frequent light feedings of a complete fertilizer such as fish emulsion.

Bird's Nest Fern

12-48" • Strong indirect light

Glossy individual fronds, apple green with black ribs, unfurl from heart of plant. Tough enough to summer outdoors on a shady patio if protected from direct sunlight.

Five-Finger Fern

1-3' • Shade

Lacy fronds fork to make a fingerlike pattern atop thin 1 to 2½-foot stems. Adds an airy, fresh touch to other cool loving plants such as begonias, fuchsias, and azaleas.

Lace Fern, Japanese

1-3' • Shade

Handsomely symmetrical with dense, finely cut fronds, Japanese lace fern is an easy plant to grow for a shady corner of the garden. Growth is upright and somewhat spreading; fronds are darkest green.

Maidenhair Fern

1-3' • Moderate indirect light or shade

Fragile-looking fern suitable for house or greenhouse year-round, or outdoors during summer in sheltered patio area. Bright green, finely cut fronds grow on wiry, almost black stems. Maidenhairs can be temperamental—constant moisture and frost protection are essential.

Squirrel's Foot Fern

12-30" • Moderate indirect light

Best in a hanging basket, this fern has finely divided fronds to 12 inches long, curving downward; furry rhizomes resembling squirrels' feet creep over soil surface and container. Outdoors in mild spring, summer; otherwise indoors.

Sword Fern

1-4' • Strong indirect light

Variety of popular favorites among *Nephrolepis exaltata* include Boston fern (*N. e.* 'Bostoniense'), Roosevelt fern (*N. e.* 'Rooseveltii'), and *N. e.* 'Whitmanii'. All are easy to grow indoors in bright indirect light with regular fertilizing, ample moisture, and some humidity. Can be summered outdoors if protected.

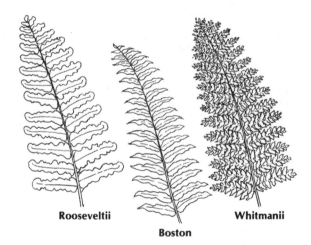

Rooseveltii   **Whitmanii**

Boston

Tree Ferns

3-20' • Filtered sun

Located in a prominent spot, dramatic tree ferns need no help from other plants to be effective. Most are quite hardy, even where light frost occurs.

Australian tree fern. Broad arching fronds are finely cut, bright green, often up to 10 feet long. Fast growing.

Hawaiian tree fern. Sometimes reaching 6 feet high, 8 feet wide; has feathery, golden green fronds.

Tasmanian tree fern. Characterized by a thick, fuzzy, red brown trunk and dark green, arching fronds to 6 feet long. Slow growing, but the hardiest of the tree ferns.

Dependable succulents and cacti

Of all possible plants suited for container gardening, none are more diversified or offer the particular intrigue found with succulents and cacti. Both are easy to grow and propagate, requiring little maintenance for healthy, active growth. Their chief need is good drainage, so provide them with a fast-draining soil in pots that also drain easily.

In general, succulents need more water than cacti, but in both cases apply sparingly. Even in the summer many get by with one watering a week. In cool areas, water just enough to keep plants from shriveling. Fertilize only during the growing period.

Out of the tremendous number of different kinds of succulents and cacti, we have listed a few favored for their foliage, flowers, or form.

Aeonium

6–36" • Sun or filtered sun

Extremely decorative group of shrubby plants characterized by woody stems crowned with rosettes of fleshy leaves. *A. decorum* has reddish-tinged leaves; *A. arboreum* has tall clusters of yellow flowers; *A. simsii*, widely sold, forms a cushion of bright green rosettes. All are best along the coast or in mild inland areas.

Agave Attenuata

3–8' • Filtered sun

An imposing container plant: 2-foot-long spineless leaves and a 5-foot trunk bearing greenish yellow flowers on arching stems. Best in rich soil with ample water; needs protection from frost and hottest sun.

Aloe

1–10' • Sun

There is a kind of aloe to bloom in every month of the year, but the biggest show is from February to September. Varying from 6-inch miniatures to 10-foot trees, aloes form clumps of fleshy, pointed, often banded leaves and clusters of red, orange, or yellow flowers. Easy to grow in frost-free areas.

How to graft cactus

There are three grafting methods: flat, cleft, and side. The flat graft—easiest for rounded scions—fits a flat base to a flat top. The cleft graft is good for flat scions like epiphyllum because it fits a wedge-shaped base into a "v" cut. The third method is a side graft, in which both plants are cut on a slant and respective pieces joined with string until a union is formed. Long, slender scions are best handled this way.

Here are four easy steps to follow: 1) With a sharp knife, slice the top off the stock plant. A second, very thin slice may be made and left in place to keep cut surface moist. 2) Trim down the shoulders of the stock. All exposed tissue of stock and scion must be perfectly clean to avoid rot. 3) Be sure inner growth rings of stock and scion are the same diameter so they will successfully unite; if rings are not matched, the graft will fail. 4) Remove thin slice (made in step 1) from stock and quickly apply scion; press them gently together. Secure scion in place with rubber bands, string, or toothpicks.

Flat graft

Cleft graft

Side graft

Christmas Cactus

1–3' • Sun or filtered sun

Spineless, drooping branches bear dozens of rosy 3-inch flowers at Christmas time. Pot in rich, porous, sandy soil, water frequently, and feed with liquid fertilizer as often as every 2 weeks. Give plants sun in autumn and winter, bright light the rest of the year.

Crab Cactus

1–2' • Sun

Related to Christmas cactus, crab cactus has jointed branches with two large teeth at end. Flowers, white through orange and red, bloom in winter and early spring. For care, see Christmas cactus, above.

Crassula

1–6' • Sun or filtered sun

Dependable, versatile, yet not too spectacular. Like most crassulas, jade plant *(C. argentea)* will stay compact in a small container for years, but even little plants have stout trunks and limbs like dwarf trees. *C. falcata* reaches 4 feet when fully grown, producing dense clusters of scarlet blooms in late summer. Upright form of *C. tetragona* resembles a miniature pine tree. All need sunshine for profuse blooming.

Dudleya

2–12" • Sun

Best-known is *D. brittonii.* Striking appearance includes rosettes of fleshy leaves covered with a heavy coat of chalky white powder. The stem gradually lengthens to a stout trunk. Locate in sun for best growth.

Easter Lily Cactus, see Sea Urchin Cactus

Echeveria

2–30" • Sun

Attractive, overlapped fleshy leaves grow in rosettes. Hen and chicks *(E. elegans)* has tight, grayish white rosettes, and pink and yellow flowers in spring. *E. setosa* has 4-inch-wide, dark green rosettes covered with stiff white hairs; flowers are red.

Felt Plant, see Kalanchoe Beharensis

Haworthia

6–24" • Filtered sun

All are excellent container subjects when located in partial shade. Some varieties resemble small aloes; others make little towers of neatly stacked, fleshy leaves. Leaf color ranges from grayish through shades of green.

Kalanchoe Beharenis (Felt Plant)

3–5' • Sun or filtered sun

Triangular leaves are furry, crimped on edges. In mild climates, felt plant is safe outdoors if protected from frost; elsewhere, consider it an indoor/outdoor container plant. Enjoys ample moisture.

Opuntia

2–8' • Sun

This genus includes prickly pears, beaver tail, and chollas; it divides into two groups—plants with flat, broad joints and plants with cylindrical joints. Flowers are pale green, yellow, or white marked with lavender. Hardy, will withstand both hot and cold temperatures.

Peruvian Old Man Cactus

1–5' • Sun

Handsome, columnar cactus with bristly thorns concealed in long white hair that covers the plant. Tubular pink blooms appear in May or June. Protect from hard frosts.

Sea Urchin Cactus (Easter Lily Cactus)

2–36" • Sun or filtered sun

Small cylindrical cactus, easy to grow, bears large, free-blooming flowers in summer. Use as a house plant in severe climate areas, outdoors elsewhere. Provide plenty of light, frequent feeding, and fast-draining soil.

Sansevieria

1–4' • Sun, filtered sun, or shade

Thick, banded leaves radiate up from base. Leaves of *S.* 'Hahnii' are blunt triangles; *S. trifasciata* has stiff sword leaves. Grows in poor light, seldom needs repotting, and withstands dry air and infrequent watering.

Sedum

1–6' • Sun or filtered sun

From tiny and trailing to bushy and upright, many varieties are available. Larger kinds, such as *S. oxypetalum* and *S. spectabile,* are attractive alone in pots. The lower, creeping types combine well with some larger succulents. Donkey tail sedum and *S. sieboldii* are unusual hangers.

Sempervivum Tectorum

8–24" • Sun

Nicknamed "hen and chickens," this succulent has rosettes of leaves with reddish brown, bristle-pointed tips. Needs sun and good drainage; give it ample moisture during hot summer months.

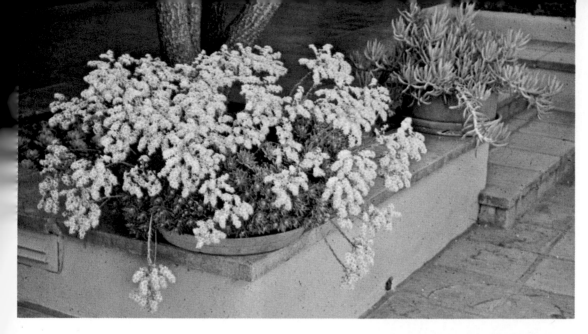

Yellow blooms *of* Aeonium floribunda *make spectacular display on patio.*

Assortment *of cacti in handmade ceramic pots.*

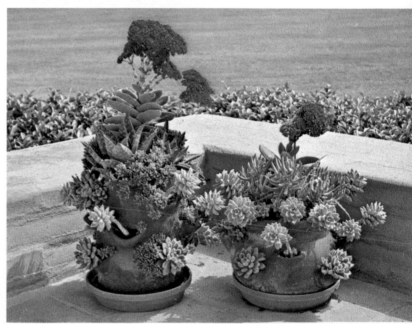

Patio corner *shows off strawberry jars of flowering succulents.*

Hardy Crassula perfossa *spills over pot's edge.*

Succulents/cacti 75

Extend your garden upward with vines

To dress up a wall, camouflage a fence, or decorate a post, or wherever a planting of some height is needed, guiding a vine to grow in a particular pattern may be the ideal solution. Even with a limited amount of actual ground space, a vine in a container, trained on a trellis or a wire frame, can be an effective portable screen. You can base your selection on color, leaf pattern, flowers, fragrance, or growing habit. Some climbers have twining stems or tendrils that attach themselves to almost anything; others need to be tied or supported.

Most vines do well in basic potting soil with ample moisture and fertilizer. It's a good idea to put in the trellis, stake, or other support when you plant. To encourage bushiness and help train your vine, pinch back main stems occasionally during active growth.

Black-Eyed Susan Vine

6' • Spring bloom • Sun

Orange, yellow, or white tubular flowers with deep purple throats cover this rapid-growing annual vine. Excellent as a portable screen or barrier when trained

Scarlet runner bean vines *in window boxes create leafy curtain outside kitchen window.*

on a wide trellis and placed in a sunny location. Massive blooming occurs in midspring, but flowers appear intermittently throughout year when encouraged by monthly feedings of complete fertilizer.

Canary-Bird Flower, see Nasturtium

Cardinal Climber

20' • Summer, autumn bloom • Sun

Related to the morning glories, this colorful annual or perennial vine is useful as a quick, temporary screen. Clustered funnel-shaped flowers are bright red (occasionally white); leaves are finely divided into slender threads. Hard-coated seeds should be soaked in warm water or notched with a knife before planting.

Clematis

6-10' • Spring, summer bloom • Filtered sun

Deciduous and free-flowering, clematis hybrids with their thick foliage and interesting blooms adapt easily to container life. Using a deep container, cover the root ball with 2 inches of soil. Put in support—wooden stakes or open wire frames—and apply a mulch to keep roots cool. Needs constant moisture and monthly feeding during growth. Great choices are *C. lawsoniana* 'Henryi', with 8-inch white blooms and dark stamens, and the evergreen, fragrant *C. armandii.*

Cup-and-Saucer Vine

10-20' • Spring, summer bloom • Sun

Pendulous bell-shaped flowers, turning from green to rosy purple, grow on graceful foot-long stems. Perennial vine vigorously grows to 20 feet, attaching its tendrils to supports. Seeds can be started indoors as early as March or sown directly into permanent containers once danger of frost has passed.

Fatshedera Lizei

6' • No bloom • Filtered sun or shade

Shrubby evergreen vine with 8-inch, ivylike foliage. Suitable both indoors and out, it tolerates partial shade but needs protection from drying winds. Plant is heavy—sturdy supports are needed. If growth gets out of hand, pinch tips to encourage side branching or prune back almost to the crown.

Ivy

3-15' • No bloom • Sun or filtered sun

Dependable, neat, uniform, evergreen—what better description for *Hedera helix?* Foliage is green or variegated, lobed or pointed, depending on the kind. Grows in sun or part shade (needs shade in hot interior areas); give it lots of water during hot seasons. Popular climbing varieties are *H. h.* 'Jubilee' and 'Bulgaria'.

Jasmine

4–20' • Winter, spring, or summer bloom • Sun or filtered sun

Valued for its strong fragrance and delightful flowers—white or golden yellow on vining varieties. Good container choices include 10-foot angelwing jasmine (*Jasminum nitidum*) with pinwheel flowers, Arabian jasmine (*J. sambac*), hardy winter jasmine (*J. nudiflorum*), and star jasmine (*Trachelospermum jasminoides*—not a true jasmine) with waxy white flowers.

Moonflower

10–25' • Summer bloom • Filtered sun

Cover an arbor or trellis with fast-growing summer shade from a container filled with moonflower vines. Heart-shaped leaves surround white, fragrant, night-blooming blossoms. Often mixed with traditional favorite 'Heavenly Blue' morning glory. Before planting in spring, soak seeds in warm water a few days to soften.

Morning Glory

5–15' • Summer, autumn bloom • Sun

Trumpetlike blooms are blue, white, red, or lavender; leaves are lobed and heart-shaped. Because seedlings don't transplant well, presoaked seeds should be planted directly into permanent containers. Water moderately and avoid fertilizing (except for Imperial Japanese morning glory, which needs rich soil and regular feeding).

Profuse blooms of lantana, ivy geraniums pour out of planters atop arbor.

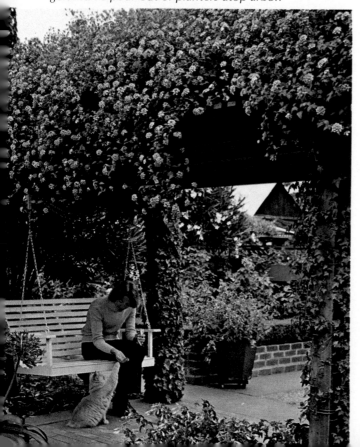

Nasturtium (Canary-Bird Flower)

10' • Summer, autumn bloom • Filtered sun

A few seeds planted in light shade in early spring grow quickly into a hardy vine covered with fringed yellow flowers. Given support for its twining stalks, it can reach 10 feet or more. Moist soil—preferably well-drained and somewhat sandy—is a must for lush, rich green foliage.

Scarlet Kadsura

3–15' • Summer bloom • Sun

Fast-growing to 15 feet, this twining evergreen perennial changes appearance with each season— white summer flowers, reddish autumn leaves, scarlet winter berries. Try planting a few seedlings at the base of a sturdy support, or train vines up a trellis or arbor. Thrives in full sun, except in hottest areas; needs pruning for shape in spring.

Scarlet Runner Bean

3–15' • Summer bloom • Sun

Slender clusters of showy red flowers are followed by dark, edible bean pods that are tasty when young. For quick shade on porches or patios, try training vines up strings suspended from overhang. Plant seeds in late spring, giving them full sun and ample moisture.

Sweet Pea

3–9' • Summer bloom • Filtered sun

Bluish green foliage and delightfully fragrant rose-colored flowers characterize perennial sweet pea climber *Lathyrus latifolius*. Grow vigorous vines with a long blooming period (June to September) by watering often and fertilizing monthly.

Potted ivy trains up arch-shaped wire frames. For ease, portability, frames pull apart.

Festive ways to use container plants

. . . as gifts

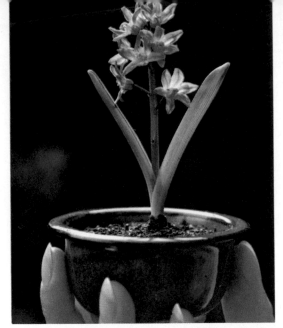

Glory-of-the-snow *just 6 inches high.*

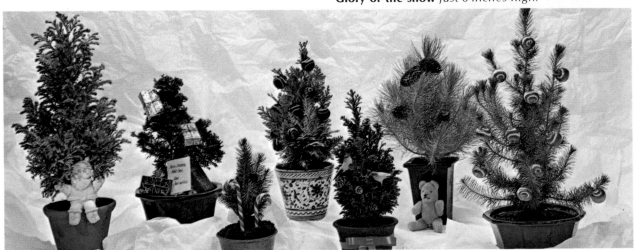

Miniature evergreens *are potted, then decorated for the ultimate in holiday gift giving.*

Small *Colorado spruce sparkles with pinpoint lights.*

. . . as decorations

Bonsai *chrysanthemum centerpiece.*

Index

Photographers

George J. Ball, Inc.: 15 top. **Robert Bander:** 10 top right.
Kathleen Norris Brenzel: 16 top, 17 top right.
Clyde Childress: 8 all. **Glenn Christiansen:** 7 top, 17
lower left, 59 left, 61, 62 lower right, 78 lower right.
Roger Flanagan: 46 top. **Gerald R. Fredrick:** 34 all, 38,
77 lower left. **Dorothy Krell:** 7 center left and right,
bottom, 10 top left, lower right, 12 all, 13 lower, 15
lower left, 48 top right, lower, 52 top, lower right, 53
top, lower right, 54 top left, lower left and right, 60
lower right, 70 lower left. **Roy Krell:** 5 top. **Peggy Kuhn:**
77 right. **Ells Marugg:** 2, 4, 10 center right, lower left,
13 top, 16 lower left, 40 all, 41 all, 43 all, 48 top left,
51 all, 54 top right, 59 right, 60 left, top right, 62 lower
left, 67 top left and right, 68, 69 all, 70 top left and
lower right, 75 all, 78 lower left. **Don Normark:** 46
lower left, upper right, 67 lower left, 70 top right, 76.
Norman A. Plate: 5 lower left and right, 16 lower
right, 17 lower right, 18, 46 lower right, 53 lower left,
62 top right, 67 lower right. **Darrow Watt:** 17 top left,
30, 62 top left, 78 top and center, **Peter O. Whiteley:**
52 lower left.